FERNAND LÉGER

TEXT BY

WERNER SCHMALENBACH

TRANSLATED BY ROBERT ALLEN, WITH JAMES EMMONS

HARRY N. ABRAMS, INC., PUBLISHERS, NEW YORK

1090 8KF FO2 19.95
ISBN 0–8109–1263–5

Library of Congress Catalog Card Number: 85–71495
Published in 1985 by Harry N. Abrams, Incorporated, New York
Also published in a leatherbound edition for The Easton Press,
Norwalk, Connecticut. All rights reserved. This is a concise edition of
Werner Schmalenbach's Léger, originally published in 1976. No part
of the contents of this book may be reproduced without the written
permission of the publishers.
Picture reproduction rights reserved by S.P.A.D.E.M., Paris
Printed and bound in Japan

CONTENTS

The new century was dawning when Fernand Léger, son of a Norman cattle breeder, reached Paris in 1900. He was nineteen years old and had served an apprenticeship of just two years with an architect at Caen. In Paris, too, he worked in an architect's office for a start. It was only in 1903, after finishing his military service at Versailles, that Léger entered the École des Arts Décoratifs and began to attend the celebrated Académie Julian, having failed to pass the entrance examination at the École des Beaux-Arts. At the same time he earned a precarious living working as an architectural draftsman and retouching photographs on the side. In 1905 he fell ill, owing to his miserable living conditions, and spent the winter recuperating in Corsica. Although Léger subsequently destroyed most of his early work, a few paintings done in the period 1904–5 are still extant.

Picasso was the same age as Léger and, like him, arrived in Paris in 1900. But he was immediately caught up in and branded by the artistic life of the metropolis and only a few years later was one of its decisive forces. Léger, on the other hand, remained quite untouched by what was in the air at the time. In 1905 the Fauves created a sensation at the Salon d'Automne, and Léger, with his life-long obsession with color, ought to have been attracted and influenced, then, if not earlier, by their pure, strong colors. But there is no sign of Fauvist influence in his paintings, and even his writings reflect a lack of interest in the Fauves. In fact, it was Impressionism—though long past its prime—that was the first liberating influence he felt.

Léger's debt to the Impressionists is evident in *My Mother's Garden* of 1905 (fig. 3), a rather nondescript, impersonal painting in the late Impressionist manner with bright accents dotted about in a greenish color scheme and with loose, comma-like brushstrokes. But the question of autonomous color was posed here, and the foundations of a solid composition were laid. Indeed, the juxtaposition of straight lines and circles, so important in his later work, is already clear. In the few landscapes Léger painted on that first trip to Corsica, the flaky handling, the "virgulism," of the Impressionists gives way to a firmer, more emphatic structure. One is tempted to recognize the first influence of Cézanne, forty-two of whose works had been shown at the Salon d'Automne of 1907; Cézanne died in 1906, when Léger was twenty-five years old.

1. SELF-PORTRAIT. c. 1930. Ink, 9 1/2 × 6 1/4".
Musée National Fernand Léger, Biot

Léger said many years later that Impressionism was the major revolution in modern times because it put an end to chiaroscuro. He himself had started out by painting after the manner of the Impressionists but had soon realized that their age, unlike his own, had been a "melodious" one. This statement is typical of Léger, in whose writings the antimelodious principle crops up in different terms again and again. He called Cézanne "the transitional artist between modern painters and Impressionism" and confessed that it had taken three years for him to break free from Cézanne's influence.

It was owing to that influence that Léger first pursued form instead of color, associating himself with the Cubists instead of the Fauves. This was an act of self-denial, particularly since he had already discovered and employed uninhibited color; moreover, it required an all the more intense concentration on the problems of form, which was necessary if he was to unite form and color in a new pictorial language. Under Cézanne's impact and already within the sphere of influence of the Cubist experiment, Léger submitted to the stern demands of form.

The pictures he painted about 1909–10 bear witness to this first exercise in form. A good example is *Woman Sewing* (fig. 5), in which the human figure and all its limbs and parts are petrified in massive angular forms, while every trace of atmospheric and spiritual factors has disappeared and color, subdued almost to the point of monochromy, yields place to form. Obviously, this sort of painting is based on Cézanne's urgent appeal for form. But Léger went a great deal further: abandoning Cézanne's painterly touches of color, he aimed at a new, robust, monumental solidity.

In 1907 Picasso's *Les Demoiselles d'Avignon* had ushered in the Cubist movement. In 1909 what is known as the Analytic phase of Cubism was at its peak. Although Léger's *Woman Sewing* shows hardly a sign of its influence, his *Table and Fruit* (fig. 6) is far too closely akin to Analytic Cubism to have been produced quite independently of it. Table and bowl are disintegrated and the fragments have a crystalline structure. The geometrization of the tablecloth foreshadows Léger's pictures of 1911–12.

More significant than the closeness of this still life to Cubism is the distance from Cubism, and what one might call the total independence, of *Nudes in the Forest* (colorplate 1). Léger started on this first important work in 1909 and finished it the following year. It shows a mighty mass of coarse-cut forms, a primeval chaos from which nude male figures—woodcutters among the trees—gradually emerge. What may be termed Léger's personal brand of Cubism has little in common with that of Picasso and Braque. In both form and subject this painting is far removed from Cubism proper; the rigorous solidity of the forms and the theme of the workers make it already a typical Léger. What is not yet altogether typical is the attitude toward color: the picture is painted in soft tones ranging from gray-green to brown-purple, unbroken by any vivid color accents.

In this work Léger broke resolutely with the "melodious" manner of the Impressionists. The air-light continuum—the equivalent of Impressionism's color continuum—has been burst open and replaced by a discontinuity that pervades the entire composition, the individual figures, and even the tree trunks. Forms jostle each other. This too is typical Léger and also one of the essential principles of early twentieth-century art insisted on by Fauves and Cubists alike. The former abolished the color continuum, the latter the form continuum. Both groups set up a formal counterforce against all that is organic. The decisive event of their generation was not liberation from the imitation of nature but their assault on the organic homogeneity of nature.

In accordance with this principle, the nude woodcutters in Léger's big forest picture are built up of independent elements that function not organically but mechanically, after the manner of robots. This view of the human figure seems to have been prepared for by Léger in a series of pen drawings he did between 1905 and 1911. They show man as a violent congeries of limbs combined without the slightest trace of physical harmony. Unity is obtained not by the organic flow of lines but by the dynamic temperament of the draftsman. In their novel rhythm these nude drawings are not far removed from Picasso's *Les Demoiselles d'Avignon*.

When *Nudes in the Forest* was exhibited at the Salon des Indépendants of 1911, it caused a great stir. All of a sudden Léger found himself the focal point of the young artistic movement in Paris. In 1908, after other stays in Corsica, he had taken a studio in the legendary "Ruche" in Montparnasse near the slaughterhouses of Vaugirard. At that time or slightly later, painters like Delaunay, Chagall, and Soutine lived there too, as did sculptors like Archipenko, Laurens, and Lipchitz; and

2. SELF-PORTRAIT. 1946. Ink, 7 7/8 × 5 1/4". Galerie Berggruen, Paris

3. MY MOTHER'S GARDEN. 1905. Oil on canvas,
18 1/8 × 15". Musée National Fernand Léger, Biot

writers like Guillaume Apollinaire, Max Jacob, Pierre Reverdy, Blaise Cendrars, and Maurice Raynal were frequent visitors. Léger and Cendrars became lifelong friends. Through Robert Delaunay, the painter closest to him, Léger met Henri Rousseau le Douanier, whom he called on often and whose work he greatly admired. Rousseau's influence on Léger can be seen occasionally even in his latest pictures. In 1910 the dealer Daniel-Henry Kahnweiler took Léger under his wing, thus admitting him to the inner circle of the Cubists, but the two "camps"—Montmartre and Montparnasse—did not mix. Léger mostly frequented Jacques Villon's studio at Puteaux, where he met Gleizes, Metzinger, La Fresnaye, Le Fauconnier, Kupka, Picabia, Marcel Duchamp, and others. He was closer to that circle, which founded the Section d'Or in 1912, than to Picasso's, since the classical norm to which the group subscribed, at least in its self-chosen name, answered better to Léger's nature than the Cubists' "shattering of form." An event that made a great impact on Léger's thought and work was the exhibition of the Italian Futurists in the Galerie Bernheim in Paris that same year.

What characterized Léger's art during the time that elapsed between 1910 and the outbreak of

4. CORSICAN VILLAGE
AT SUNSET. 1905.
Oil on canvas,
19 1/2 × 25 1/2".
Private collection

World War I was his encounter with Cubism. Picasso and Braque developed the Cubist manner of painting in an almost identical fashion; Léger, instead, went his own way. What distinguished him from the others was an untiring search for solid form, a stubborn insistence on the concrete, and the refusal to give up color entirely for monochromy. But Léger must be looked at in the context of the group: before abandoning Cubism, he made an essential contribution to it. In *The Wedding* of 1910–11 (colorplate 2) he produced one of the finest examples of classic Cubism. The large picture bears witness to the drama of his adaptation to the movement. Although he has adopted the Cubists' rhythmic scheme and their fragmentation of figures and objects, the figurative element— already composed of the tubular forms typical of Léger—still asserts itself. In addition, large geometric planes and strong color accents contrast with the Cubist-Futurist shattering of forms. These opposing forces give the picture a dynamic quality that is typical of Léger but quite untypical of Cubism, being due, rather, to the impact of Futurism.

The process thus started continued and can be traced almost step by step through 1911 and 1912. The color grows stronger and more significant. Intensely contrasted patches of color impinge more

5. WOMAN SEWING. c. 1910. Oil on canvas, 28 3/8 × 21 1/4″. Private collection, Paris

6. TABLE AND FRUIT. 1909. Oil on canvas, 33 × 38 7/8″. The Minneapolis Institute of Arts. William Hood Dunwoody Fund

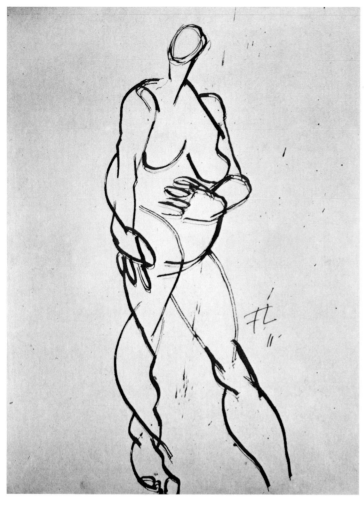

left: 7. NUDE. 1911. Ink, 13 × 9 7/8″. Private collection

right: 8. STUDY OF A NUDE. 1912. Ink, 11 3/4 × 7 7/8″. Musée National d'Art Moderne, Paris. Gift of D.-H. Kahnweiler

and more dynamically on the throng of still pale-colored forms. The geometric character of the individual forms becomes clearer and more obvious. The development is palpable when one studies the major works Léger produced during that period—*The Wedding* (1910–11), *The Smokers* (1911; colorplate 3), and *Woman in Blue* (two versions, 1912; colorplate 4). In the third of these paintings broad elemental forms in luminous colors dominate the fragmentary Cubist structure, from which such objects as a chairback or a tabletop with tableware emerge. With the large form of the woman herself Léger attained what was for him the acme of abstraction.

For all their masterly beauty, these three pictures give one the impression—perhaps shared by the artist himself—that concentration on exclusively formal problems had put him out of touch with reality, so that he now needed to approach nature from a new angle. A picture like the landscape of 1912 in Vienna (colorplate 5) tells us much about this need. The Cubist schema is abandoned and

Cubist principles are applied more freely in a landscape in which nature comes into her own. Quiet, unspectacular, undemonstrative paintings of this sort are like moments of relaxation next to and after the intense formalism of his major Cubist works.

Between 1912 and 1914 Léger took a decisive step that led him to abandon the Cubist model definitively and to adopt an absolutely personal Cubism of his own—the "tubism" that owes its ironical name to the tube and pipe shapes on which it is based. The result was a number of Contrasts of Forms (see colorplate 9, fig. 12), stairways (see colorplate 8, fig. 13), women in easy chairs, and village scenes (see colorplates 6, 7). The picture-puzzle quality of Léger's classic Cubist works has given way to a straightforward figuration. A tree is a tree, a house is a house. On the formal level, a sphere is a sphere, a cube a cube, a cylinder a cylinder. On the color level, red is red and blue is blue. All this tallies with the artistic philosophy that Léger began to set forth in his many writings at that time.

The Contrasts of Forms series and the paintings that followed closely in their wake were the first conclusive embodiments of the theory of contrasts that from then on was the main thread of Léger's writings. He insisted that forms and colors should be placed side by side, isolated from and contrasting with each other; he believed there was no other way to raise them to their highest power and make them most effective. Once again, discontinuity in place of the organic continuum. Color transitions, he said, weaken stored-up energy no less than formal harmony. Léger emphatically opposed these "tubist" works, with their virulent contrasts of forms and colors, to the cultivated, "tasteful" painting that he abominated his whole life long. His pictures tended to be static, but the principle of "multiplicative contrast" gave them enormous rhythmic liveliness, activity, and dynamism. The

dynamism that Léger never tired of insisting upon is achieved by the constantly contrasted handling, whereas the staticity that he demanded no less insistently is left to the strictly articulated composition. Staticity and dynamism do not contradict each other in his work, as evidenced by the pictures he painted in 1913 and 1914.

In those pictures he professed for the first time his unreserved faith in color. In this connection one is tempted to see in Léger a sort of Fauvist Cubism—a version of Cubism that does not exist in Picasso, Braque, or Juan Gris. Léger did not find his artistic way until he could pronounce the word "color" without reservation. There is hardly another outstanding twentieth-century painter in whose work the idea of color impinges on our consciousness with such force as in Léger's—that is, since the phase of 1912–14

9. HOUSES UNDER THE TREES. 1913. Oil on canvas, 28 3/4 × 36 1/4". Private collection

that was so decisive for his art. In spite of this, one hesitates to count him among the great colorists of his day, such as Pierre Bonnard or Paul Klee, who in very different ways extracted from colors an incredible richness and magic. By comparison Léger's colors are primitive, undifferentiated, superficial, and crude. To borrow a term from the vocabulary of another art, one might call them "prosy." Nothing is more alien to Léger than the "musicality" and "poetry" of colors: his are sober, matter-of-fact, and no psychic or atmospheric factors veil their elemental clarity. They are as evident as the colors used for traffic signals. This is even truer of pictures later than those of 1913–14, which still display a certain temperamental, painterly character. But at the same time their festive luminosity raises them far above the mere quality of color to a level where their combinations produce a rich, polyphonic composition.

Fernand Léger's colors have neither transparency nor transcendence. Being mostly primary, they conceal nothing and symbolize nothing. Their nature is physical rather than psychic, sensory rather than intellectual. They are used less for self-expression—for which the artist felt no need—than to enable the painting and the objects represented in it to make a certain pictorial statement. They belong to the "objective" world of the picture.

Like all his generation except the Surrealists, what Léger wanted above all was to free the color from the object, to make the color independent. But this is only one aspect of the problem. No less important, and certainly more personal, was the new relationship of color to object. From now on, throughout his entire oeuvre, Léger chose his colors autocratically, without a thought to local color; nonetheless, they are clearly linked with the objects represented—houses, roofs, trees, or what have you. As a result, color has the dual function of providing rhythm and characterization: it must satisfy the demands of both the picture and the objects it contains.

The figurative factor attains a new significance. For a striking example of this, compare *Woman in Blue* of 1912 (colorplate 4) and the women in easy chairs of 1914 (see fig. 10). The later paintings employ far simpler means of expression and are

10. WOMAN IN RED AND GREEN. 1914. Oil on canvas, 39 1/2 × 31 7/8". Musée National d'Art Moderne, Paris

11. THE FOURTEENTH OF JULY. 1914. Oil on canvas, 28 3/4 × 23 5/8". Musée National Fernand Léger, Biot

12. CONTRAST OF FORMS. 1913. Gouache, 19 3/4 × 14 5/8″. Galerie Beyeler, Basel

13. THE STAIRCASE (2nd state). 1914. Oil on canvas, 35 × 49 1/4". Collection Harold Diamond, New York City

also far more representational. Every form can be recognized at once for the thing it represents, though the representational details are reduced to a minimum. And because of their solid volumes all the forms have the character of objects or fragments of objects. But at the same time abstraction has reached a very advanced stage: the figures are made up of volumes that are barely characterized. For this reason, the appearance of the totally abstract Contrasts of Forms, with their tubular and therefore substantive elements, more or less simultaneous with the seated women, the stairways, and the village scenes did not indicate a break with the past. Compared with these nonrepresentational pictures, earlier works like *The Wedding* or *Woman in Blue*, though more figurative in theme, seem more abstract—concerned with the problems of abstraction rather than with the problems of figure and object. In the works Léger did in 1913 and 1914 the contradiction between representational and nonrepresentational has been superbly overcome.

Léger directed all his energy to the picture as an aspect of reality *sui generis* and never tired of insisting that objects and figures be looked upon and treated merely as pictorial values. Yet in his works, more clearly than in those of Picasso and Braque, objects preserve their individual character, though, needless to say, they are not naturalistically portrayed. Even "abstract" colored forms are transmuted into solid, stable, stereometric objects. Again and again he demanded that "pure" forms be treated as actual things—spheres, cones, or cylinders, in accordance with Cézanne's age-old pronouncement—and beyond that, as volumes possessing a well-defined reality content. To the Cubists' increasing negation of reality Léger opposed a new affirmation of reality—his "new realism," which comprised the concrete value of form and color and of objects and fragments of objects, and a profession of faith in the modern world of workers and machines that was already mirrored in the tubular forms of his Contrasts of Forms. His glorification of technical or

16

technoid objects contrasts sharply with the Cubists' preference for properties borrowed from artistic circles, such as guitars, mandolins, pipes, and brandy glasses. In Picasso and Braque we find the emblems of an artistic culture; in Léger, the emblems of our modern civilization.

Thus Léger, while putting a great distance between himself and nature, was justified in speaking of a new realism. In his writings he distinguished between visual realism—it might be more correctly termed naturalism—and conceptual realism. Applied to his art, this means that the intellectual concept is not antirealistic but is turned toward reality; the content of the reality lies not in visual conformity but in grasp, and is strengthened by the technicality of the object forms. For here reality also signifies topicality and depends as much on references to the modern environment as it does on the artistic idiom employed. Consequently, one might say that the very use of modern form patterns represents a facet of realism; and it is in this sense that Léger repeatedly stated that where the picture is concerned realism consists in the interaction of the three great pictorial mediums—line, color, and form.

The two years 1913 and 1914 that immediately preceded the war were the decisive, fertile period during which Léger attained his own personal,

14. SOLDIERS IN A DUGOUT. 1915. Ink, 7 1/2 × 5 1/4". Private collection, London

15. Study for THE CARDPLAYERS. 1916. Ink, 6 3/4 × 7 7/8". Private collection, U.S.A.

16. THE BARGE. 1917.
Gouache, 6 3/4 × 9 1/2″.
Private collection

independent expression. Everything he had done before, including some already outstanding works, seems to have been in preparation for this moment of liberation. The encounter with Cubism, not instituted by him but reflected in his paintings from *The Wedding* to *Woman in Blue*, was behind him. He cast off its fetters and, in opposition to the Cubism of Picasso, set up a totally different brand that has been given the label "Colorful Cubism"—far too weak a term and reminiscent of Delaunay's "Orphism." In fact, its decisive feature is not its colorfulness but its resolute insistence on the object and on the reality of the modern world. It also displays a unity of staticity and dynamism, laid down by Léger in his theory of contrasts and realized in his painting since 1909–10.

In 1914 Léger was thirty-three years old. In the works painted during the last prewar years his art had achieved both force and feeling. Solid, healthy, reliable, far removed from the aesthetic lyricism displayed by Picasso and Braque at that time—one is tempted to call it "masculine." Léger's thirst for form and color is apparently stilled; not so his thirst for reality. It is idle to ask how his art would have evolved had the war not brought it to a standstill. We may, however, presume that the liberated, independent forms would have ap-

proached still closer to reality. But war came, and it produced an interlude which for Léger was more than a matter of time.

War brought to the artist a new, stunning experience of reality that ranged from the revelation of the metallic forms of gun barrels to the discovery of the "simple people" and the brotherhood of mankind that he had previously ignored. "It was at war," he said later, "that I got my two feet on the ground. . . ."

I left Paris in a period of abstraction, of pictorial liberation. Without any transition I found myself shoulder to shoulder with the entire French nation; assigned to the sappers, my new buddies were miners, laborers, wood- and ironworkers. . . . At the same time I was dazzled by the breechblock of a 75 mm gun opened in the sun, the magic of light on polished metal. That was just what it took to make me forget the abstract art of 1912–13. . . . Since I got my teeth into that reality the object has never left me. The breechblock of that 75 mm gun opened in the sun taught me more for my artistic evolution than all the museums in the world.

Even so, it is safe to say that Léger would not have

Quotations of statements made by Léger are from the following publications: Fernand Léger, *Fonctions de la peinture* (Ed. Gonthier, Paris, 1965), and Roger Garaudy, *Pour un Réalisme du XX· siècle: Dialogue posthume avec Fernand Léger* (Ed. Bernard Grasset, Paris, 1968).

7. MECHANICAL ELEMENTS. 1919. Oil on canvas, 36 1/4 × 28 3/4″. Galerie Beyeler, Basel

18. THE TWO ACROBATS. 1918. Oil on canvas,
35 × 23 1/2".
Collection Norman Granz, Geneva

"seen" this gun had his eye not already been prepared for it. For tubular forms had already existed in his work before his wartime experience of gun barrels. What was completely new was meeting and making friends with simple people after the years spent in the intellectual and artistic atmosphere of Paris, where he had devoted himself to the formal problems of his art and to discussions with artists, poets, and men of letters. In 1916 he recorded this new experience in *Soldier with a Pipe* (colorplate 10), whose powerful human impression of the soldier, oblivious to all but his thoughts and his pipe, is combined with the "tubist" forms of the objects to render the somber sadness and dignity of the common man. This is undoubtedly one of the most exemplary pictures of World War I, even though, or perhaps because, it makes do without muddy trenches, exploding shells, or mangled corpses.

Just as later it was characteristic of Léger that he did not paint work so much as the break between spells of work, here he paints the break in the fighting, not the fighting itself. The same is true of *The Cardplayers* of 1917 (colorplate 11). Three soldiers have taken time out from the war to have a game of cards; though the wartime setting is there, pervading the picture, there remains no trace of a human atmosphere. By that time the war had come to an end for Léger, who had been gassed in 1916. But the gleaming gun barrels he saw at the front have had their effect on him: the tubular forms are smoother, more metallic, more technical than those of 1913–14. The human atmosphere that is so affecting in the *Soldier with a Pipe* of 1916 has given way to a world of robot-like machinery. *The Cardplayers* initiates Léger's "Mechanical Period," which covers the years 1918–20, with offshoots that continue into the early twenties.

Until now the mechanical factor had been a purely formal principle of Léger's art, as opposed to the organic and what Léger called the "melodious" principle. Small, machine-like forms appeared even in *The Wedding* of 1911, painted when Léger was closest to classic Cubism. They grew larger and coarser until they became the tubular forms of the Contrasts of Forms of 1913–14. There, however, they still preserved a certain calligraphic quality and a trace of subjectivity. But this was soon eliminated in favor of objectivity, anonymity, and mechanicality: *The Cardplayers* of 1917 is the first picture in which we find the cold, metallically polished forms that were so typical of Léger in the twenties. From now on the mechanical factor is no longer merely a formal principle but a conscious, intentional analogy to the reality of the modern world.

It offered Léger a new substance to still his hunger for reality. The subject matter of his paintings expanded to include machines and factories, mechanics and fitters, townscapes, railroad stations, and canal barges. He was fascinated by the modern world of work, and it conditioned his painting both thematically and artistically: "The world of work," as he himself said, "is the only interesting one." The scenic elements, where they still existed, were more civilized than in his villages of 1913 and 1914 (see colorplates 6, 7). And when for once he painted acrobats (see colorplate 12, fig. 18), they might just as well have been factory workers. Whereas the villages and the seated women of 1913–14 had been little more than the infrastructure of a new artistic form—neither steeples nor ladies interested Léger—his aim now was to celebrate the machine, the factory, the worker, the metropolis. Needless to say, he could not do so by representing them naturalistically. The means of expression had to be "purely" pictorial and subject to the laws of the picture. But Léger was convinced that an unbreakable link existed between the rhythm of the modern world and the autonomous rhythm of modern painting, and it was this link that he wanted to render in his art. The gears, pistons, and levers he painted do not, of course, add up to actual machines, but they do evoke the idea of technology and machinery.

For instance, the big painting of 1918 entitled *The Disks* (colorplate 13) concerns the interior of a factory, but what really counts is the functional character of the interlocking forms, the "cold" language of the brightly colored disks, the technical precision of the picture, and the dynamic rhythm of the forms before the geometric backdrop. The same is true of *Mechanical Elements* of 1918–23 (colorplate 14) with its cylindrical pieces of metal. It is not only the flashing traffic signals or the fragments of stencil letters but also the rhythmic buildup of planes that imbues *The City* of 1919–20 (colorplate 15) with the spirit of this modern reality as Léger understood it. Maybe the painter was fascinated by the metropolis and the machine because he was born in a rural environment. Townspeople are allured by a rustic romanticism; so, too, an urban romanticism may well attract those who grow up in the country.

His energetic interest in the modern urban and industrial reality brought Léger into line with other contemporary artists and authors. Chief among the latter was Blaise Cendrars; chief among the former, Robert Delaunay, whose paintings sing the praises of the Eiffel Tower, sports stadiums, airplanes, and posters. Léger was very conscious of the distance between himself and Delaunay: he would have nothing to do with the differentiated and extremely "civilized" colors of his friend's Orphism or with his concept of color as the symbol of light. Instead, he insisted on the shrill colors of the great city and the harsh staccato rhythm of the machine: his urban romanticism was infinitely unromantic.

Léger committed himself to the reality of modern life as the Italian Futurists had before him. The controversial concept of the "committed" artist has since become a subject of discussion. Although Léger's commitment was limited to what

concerns art directly—its laws, its autonomy—what he wanted was "truth" both in and outside art. No study of *art engagé* would be complete if it omitted a mention of Léger; in fact, he, rather than George Grosz, Otto Dix, or any other painter, has been named its chief exponent.

This may be explained by a comparison between Léger and his antipode, Picasso. Picasso was an incessantly creative, self-sufficient natural genius, a stupendous "sport" with a gift of phenomenal scale, a painter who needed no "ethic" to guide his inspiration. Léger's creative powers, though they too were extraordinary, do not strike one as a divine gift; they found expression in one picture after another as if by a sequence of acts of will and were based on convictions and principles. Picasso was possessed by his demons; Léger was obsessed by his duty as a painter of the present day. Picasso was a happy genius who yielded to his moods and fancies (which did not exclude hard work); Léger was a man with a mission who did not give nature a free rein but blazed "a trail for truth" in his art, his talks, and his writings—for his

19. PROPELLERS. 1918.
Oil on canvas, 31 7/8 × 25 3/4".
The Museum of Modern Art, New York City.
Katherine S. Dreier Bequest

ethic demanded more than pictures from him. In this he differed from the earliest Cubists and joined all those who, during the interwar period, identified artistic reform with social reform. In Picasso's work, for all the revolutions he provoked (but only in art) and all his manifestations of political opinion, there is not the slightest trace of this concern. His art was art for its own sake; it was born of his creative imagination and was an exact reflection of that imagination. Creative potency was the scale and content of his art. For Picasso, art was a ceaselessly renewed adventure; for Léger it was a constant, unwavering duty. True, with his *Guernica* Picasso made a spectacular entry into the discussion on *art engagé*; but this was an occasional commitment prompted by some catastrophe or other: by Guernica in 1937, by Korea in 1951. However deeply it may have affected him, an apocalyptic event was for him a unique source of artistic inspiration. Léger's commitment, on the other hand, was, from the very start and to the very end, related to the social reality of his time, from his woodcutters of 1909–10 to the construction workers of 1949–51 and attaining highest awareness in his "Mechanical Period" of 1918–20. Léger did not wail like Cassandra when dreadful things occurred; he always stood by the workers and their world, whereas Picasso associated with artists and bullfighters, harlequins and pretty women. For this reason Léger's place in the typology of the modern artist is poles apart from Picasso's: he was not a creative genius who found in himself the source of his work, but an artist who occupied a position in real life, accepted responsibilities, and set himself collective tasks.

His position compelled him to tackle disciplines outside the sphere of art. This brought him into contact with many twentieth-century artists dedi-

20. Design for the sets for LA CRÉATION DU MONDE. 1923. Gouache, 16 1/8 × 22 1/2". Musée National Fernand Léger, Biot

cated to transforming modern life in a great variety of fields—from the exponents of De Stijl in Holland to the Russian Constructivists, from the Purists in France to the Bauhaus master builders in Germany. Everywhere art abandoned the studio for the street. It was not merely a question of personal versatility but, rather, a historic obligation accepted by a great many artists, Léger among them. When he adopted Manet's demand for *contemporanéité* and said that an artist must always be "in accord with his epoch," Léger did not mean it merely as an isolated artistic attitude but as aiming for the secular transformation of the world in all its aspects.

Thus, for him as for many other artists, it was quite natural to take a lifelong interest in the new architecture. Léger dreamed of colorful cities, colorful residential quarters, colorful factories. What interested him most was the integration of the fine arts in modern buildings and, consequently, the development of a style that would have a collective validity. In 1925 he worked with Delaunay on a project by the architect Robert Mallet-Stevens for the Exhibition of Decorative Arts in Paris and did his first mural for Le Corbusier's "Esprit Nouveau" pavilion. His connection with Le Corbusier was lasting and friendly.

Léger was also interested in posters and shop windows. Both are frequently mentioned in his writings, and elements of modern typography and posterwork crop up in his pictures. Conversely, his art made an impact on French commercial art, both directly and through his pupils who went into the advertising business.

Like so many artists of his generation, Léger was tempted by the theater; he designed the sets and costumes for Rolf de Maré's Swedish Ballet, in 1922 for *Skating Rink* (music by Arthur Honegger) and in 1923 for Blaise Cendrars' *La Création du monde* (music by Darius Milhaud). His aim was to reduce the sets and dancers to elements of his scenic picture language, in a word, to "pictorial values." And therein lay for him the great fascination of the ballet—as compared with the drama, which depends for its life on the actor who transmits the words. "Everything can move," wrote Léger. "The human dimension that formerly predominated disappears, and the human being becomes a mechanism like all the rest." This mechanization of the human figure matched the general trend of the new theater of the twenties. It was also in 1922 that Oskar Schlemmer produced his *Triadische Ballett* at Weimar; but the action was—as the title implies—completely abstract, whereas the theme of *Skating Rink* was the hectic life of the modern metropolis that fascinated Léger.

But what chiefly captivated Léger and offered him new matter for his painting during those years was the cinema. In his own words, "The cinema is the machine age; the theater is the horse-and-buggy age." The cinema was a revelation for Léger because it is a mechanical product, a "trivial art" addressed to a vast, anonymous audience, and especially because it operates not with human beings but with lifeless "things." Again and again, both in his talks and in his writings, he extolled the cinema, particularly the close-up, which dwells on things and fragments of things. He regarded Chaplin, with his stereotype appearance and jerky movements, as one of the greatest of the contemporary artists. In 1921 Léger worked with Blaise Cendrars on Abel Gance's *La Roue* and in 1923 on *L'Inhumaine*. In 1924 he collaborated with Dudley Murphy and Man Ray to produce his own film, *Ballet mécanique*, the first ever made without a script. For Léger, doing without a script signified doing without a "subject" or "plot": it implied the triumph of the object. As he said later,

> It cost me ten thousand francs, an enormous sum in those days, but I was anxious to do it in order to assert the object and its plastic sufficiency. That is the relationship between the cinema and my painting. The Impressionists liquidated almost half the subject, we have done the rest. With the film I wanted to prove that fingernails and eyes are independent things that can stand alone.

That Léger now undertook to pass on his artistic convictions to other people, particularly the young, is typical of his position, which in this respect, too, contrasts sharply with Picasso's. In 1924 he set up a studio in the rue Notre-Dame-des-Champs with the Purist painter Amédée Ozenfant. Many years later, in 1932, he taught at the Académie de la Grande-Chaumière, and in 1940, after emigrating to the United States, he became a lecturer at Yale University and subsequently also at Mills College in Oakland, California.

Léger's "Mechanical Period" came to an end, though not abruptly, about 1920. From then on his works breathe a grand serenity. The dynamism and activism of his "mechanical" pictures are replaced by an architectonic austerity. Geometry

21. ANIMATED LANDSCAPE. 1921. Pencil, 10 × 14 5/8″.
Musée National Fernand Léger, Biot

receives its due even more clearly than before. Léger often said that modern man lives in a geometric environment. In the pictures of the "Mechanical Period" geometry was restricted mostly to the articulation of the background; after 1920 it became the predominant feature. Horizontals and verticals became the decisive elements of the composition. This trend, which did not constitute a peak in Léger's art, culminated in totally abstract paintings made up of rectangles, which the artist viewed as sketches for murals rather than as works of art in their own right. He thought he could tackle the decorative and collective function with non-representational means. But, despite his admiration for Piet Mondrian, he was not satisfied with total abstraction in easel painting.

With the termination of the "Mechanical Period" new themes came to the fore, which by their very nature were the antitheses of the mechanical, though Léger had already shown that they too could obey the mechanical principle. These new themes—nature and humanity—were typical of the early twenties. About 1924 they were replaced by the "thing," the commonplace object that remained his major motif until he achieved a synthesis in the second half of the decade.

Léger had neglected nature as a theme since his village pictures of 1913–14, and even then it had served mainly as a pretext for exemplifying the basic triad of "sphere, cone, and cylinder." In 1920–22 he did a number of what he called "animated landscapes," so termed because they contained human and animal figures (see color-plate 18, figs. 21–23). True, in those works nature

is denatured by references to a great many civilizing elements, such as factories, steel structures, and typographical signs. But despite the contrasts Léger employed to defy the delusions of nature, the pictures have an amazingly mild, almost bucolic lyricism. Men and beasts are painted mostly in grisaille and as a result seem more unnatural than the surrounding nature; they are mechanical figures like those found in his works of 1918–20. The Animated Landscapes are a sort of intermezzo in Léger's art of the early twenties; it was not until a decade later that he reverted to the motif of the free landscape in a different form.

The other major theme—humanity—though never entirely banned from Léger's image world prior to 1920, had been transformed into machine men and integrated in the mechanical rhythm of the picture. Now suddenly the human figures cast off their pictorial shackles, becoming the dominant motif and so to some extent the "subject," though Léger preferred to place them in thematically related groups in a scenic context. In contrast to those of the "Mechanical Period," these figures were seldom men, much less working men; rather, they were mostly women—not involved in a "modern" working process but seated, recumbent, or erect, with flowers or vessels in their hands (see figs. 24, 25). A festive, almost ceremonial, theatrical world of heroines with powerful, outsized limbs and long, wavy tresses takes shape. This was the start of a grand, figurative style with a classical character that was entirely new and formed a surprising parallel to Picasso's Neoclassicism of the same period. But whereas Picasso, for all his love of what was novel and startling, turned back to classical, archaic, and mythological regions that "are no concern of ours," Léger's female figures are at once timeless and topical—topical because of their formal style, their colorful directness, and their trivial, material environment. The triviality of faces and bodies is sublimated by the masklike stereotypy, the frontal presentation, and the layout of the entire picture plane.

In this way Léger, too, consciously accepted the great tradition of the French classicists from Poussin to Gauguin, but without the slightest trace of historicity or archaism. His loyalty to the world of his day excluded all classicistic drapes. Though the human figure is humanized, it is still marked by the machine: it belongs to an apparently soulless being, undifferentiated, unsentimental, masklike, surrounded by similarly structured forms and objects. Fundamentally, Léger allotted no more significant pictorial function to humans than to objects, plants, or landscape. But there is no denying that in these large compositions of 1920–22 humanity is the "hero" of the picture.

The objects that surround the human figures also achieve a greater significance: for instance, the arrangement of objects painted with scrupulous accuracy on the table in the foreground in *Three Women* (*Le Grand Déjeuner*) of 1921 (color-plate 19). That a still life of this type is not natu-ralistically handled but reduced to an extreme formal minimum does not prevent the common-place paraphernalia from coming into their own as objects and not merely as forms. One can see that Léger took a new pleasure in the object, or, rather, that his unquenchable thirst for reality turned away from the world of machines and pro-duction to the world of products and consumption. This heightened interest in the object, this "per-sonification" of the object, this "aesthetic" of the

22. ANIMATED LANDSCAPE. 1922.
Oil on canvas, 19 3/4 × 25 5/8".
Private collection

23. LE REPOS. 1921.
Oil on canvas, 19 3/4 × 25 5/8".
Private collection

24. WOMAN WITH A CAT. 1921. Oil on canvas, 36 1/4 × 25 5/8″. Kunsthalle, Hamburg

25. WOMAN WITH FLOWERS IN HER HAND. 1922. Oil on canvas, 28 7/8 × 45 7/8″.
Kunstsammlung Nordrhein-Westfalen, Düsseldorf

26. FIGURES IN A GARDEN. 1922. Oil on canvas, 25 5/8 × 36 1/4″.
Collection Mr. and Mrs. Allan D. Emil, New York City

isolated object—expressions that occur again and again in Léger's writings—must not be interpreted as meaning that the artist abandoned or deviated from his pictorial laws for the sake of the object. On the contrary, his language is yet more legal than before: the law of the picture governs the appearance of the object no less imperatively than that of the figure. Thanks to this formal insight, the object—tersely isolated in empty space—gains in both representational significance and abstractness.

In the mid- and late twenties, as a direct development of the big figure compositions of 1920–22, the emphasis was on still life, which attained freedom and independence consistent with the principle of the isolation and fragmentation of the object. Léger expanded his repertory by drawing and painting bowls of fruit, soda siphons, accordions, balustrades, hats, screens, keys, playing cards, and so on—solid, commonplace things, trivial things—but never, never "pretty" things like vases of flowers. Here, too, objective precision goes hand in hand with formal concision. The geometric substructure is still tangible; the dynamism of 1918–20 has disappeared. Many of these still lifes, in which well-designed, well-arranged objects are harmoniously presented, assume a decorative character, emphasized occasionally by the addition of a leafy branch, and an almost arabesque quality.

Unlike most works of Léger's "Mechanical Period," his figure pieces and Animated Landscapes of 1920–22 and the still lifes done after the mid-twenties are governed by the principle of flatness. All the elements of the composition are arranged parallel to the picture plane. This is also true of the big *City* of 1919–20 (see colorplate 15), the barges of 1920–23 (see colorplate 21) and even the still lifes painted about 1925 that face the spectator no less frontally than the women in the figure pieces. In these works frontality, geometric tautness, and flatness are just as essential as insistence on the substantiality of the objects. This explains how they could be produced at the same

27. UMBRELLA AND BOWLER. 1926. Oil on canvas, 50 1/4 × 38 3/4". The Museum of Modern Art, New York City. A. Conger Goodyear Fund

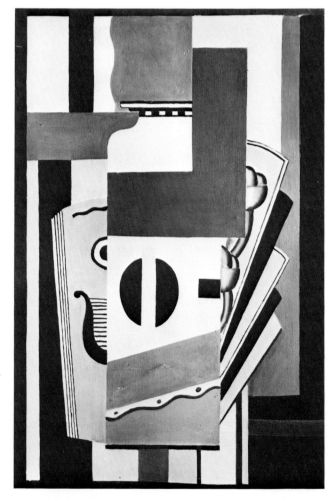

28. BOWL AND BOOK. 1926. Oil on canvas, 36 1/4 × 23 3/4". Kunsthalle, Hamburg

29. THE FRUIT BOWL. 1925. Oil on canvas, 23 × 36″. Collection James J. Shapiro, New York City

time as the series of totally unrepresentational, tautly geometrical, flat paintings that Léger executed with large wall surfaces in mind; similarly, he had produced the village and staircase pictures side by side with the abstract Contrasts of Forms of 1913–14.

About 1927 the strict arrangement begins to move. The composition is less taut, solid geometrical ties are slackened, the tyranny of the picture plane is relaxed. Suddenly the objects float free in space, though still guided by a firm hand intent on the composition. Léger now avoids the slightest trace of structural solidity; he shuns horizontals and verticals. His art breathes an entirely new rhythm, a rhythm that imbues even the female figures, which now join the still-life elements and hover in dancelike poses among the objects. Abstract forms appear more frequently and, though unrelated to reality, comport themselves like real things. Figures, objects, and abstract forms are placed side by side. The artist seems intent on juxtaposing elements that are worlds apart; the scenic context of the earlier figure compositions has disappeared entirely. But the absence of a rational, logical correlation

does not imply that the illogical, the irrational, is overly vaunted. One cannot ignore the close link with the Surrealism of that period, but in Léger it is more than a new pictorial language enriched by new possibilities of combinations and contrasts. The interplay of contrasts achieves a broader scope, but not for a second is the pictorial logic transgressed. That is why *Mona Lisa with Keys* (colorplate 27)—though not very large, the central picture of this group—is far from being proof of Léger's Surrealist intentions. The "multiplicative contrasts" between the printlike reproduction of the Mona Lisa, the bunch of keys, the sardine tin, and the abstract forms are purely pictorial contrasts, even though in this case he was doubtless counting on the appeal of an art-historical sacrilege; appeal, and not (as in Marcel Duchamp's Mona Lisa with a mustache) provocation. Léger never set out to provoke; even when he displays a social commitment, he does not criticize existing abuses but shows the ideal condition.

During the late twenties Léger seems to have felt himself in danger of becoming somehow uncommitted. In the long run he could not rest con-

30. TWO DANCERS. 1928. Oil on canvas, 36 1/4 × 28 3/4″. Collection Dr. Peter Nathan, Zurich

tent with arranging human figures, inanimate objects, and abstract forms in various combinations and causing them to float decoratively in space. Paradoxically, the more he insisted on real things, the further he found himself from reality. Concentrating on real objects instead of on reality itself, he had brought them to a suspended state in which they had lost all trace of reality. For Léger reality was a matter of men and women; it could not concern mere keys and umbrellas. True, he painted still lifes to the very end of his career. But since the great experience of World War I, man—or, rather, the common man—had been the focal point of his thinking. As if suddenly reminded of this, in 1930 (the year of *Mona Lisa with Keys*) he painted the first version of *Three Musicians*, in which the human element is at least as important as the for-

mal. The stereotype female figures of *Three Women* of 1921 are totally devoid of individual life; they belong entirely in the picture world. In the 1930 work, the three men making music together obviously belong to the common people, unlike the earlier female figures, who have no well-defined place in society. If we except the isolated *Mechanic* of 1920 (colorplate 16), here for the first time in Léger's oeuvre the common people begin to make themselves heard—typically enough, with an unmistakable reminiscence of the *peintre naïf*, Henri Rousseau. Nonetheless, this "popular" picture remains an isolated case in Léger's work, although it exists in a number of versions and the group was inserted in the 1945 variant of *The Great Parade*.

In 1931, when Léger was fifty, he went for the

31. DANCER WITH KEYS (1st state). 1929. Oil on canvas, 28 3/4 × 36 1/4″. Galerie Nathan, Zurich

32. DANCER WITH YELLOW TRIANGLE. 1930.
Oil on canvas, 25 1/2 × 21 1/4″.
Solinger Collection, New York City

33. TWO WOMEN AND THREE OBJECTS. 1936.
Oil on canvas, 51 × 63 3/4″.
Galerie Louise Leiris, Paris

34. COMPOSITION WITH TWO PARROTS. 1935–39. Oil on canvas, 157 1/2 × 169 1/4″. Musée National d'Art Moderne, Paris

first time to the United States and was fascinated by New York. From 1932 on he taught at La Grande-Chaumière, but during that time he went abroad for his first big one-man shows outside France—to Zurich in 1933, to Stockholm in 1934, to New York again in 1935. Indeed, Léger traveled a great deal during those years, until in 1940 the German invasion of France drove him to the United States for five years.

The thirties were marked chiefly by the production of the big figure pieces, *Composition with Two Parrots* (fig. 34) and *Adam and Eve* (colorplate 30). They kept him busy from 1935 to

1939, during which period he did a great many other pictures that display isolated motifs of those two major works. It is typical of Léger that he repeated certain motifs in totally different contexts; his figures are interchangeable, like properties, for he thought of them first and foremost as pictorial values and not as "subjects." On the other hand, here the "subject" gains in significance compared with the "object"; as Léger himself said, "We are witnessing a return to the grand subject. . . ." This sounds almost like a denial of his own fundamental, oft-proclaimed creed. But he never ceased to treat figures and objects as pictorial factors,

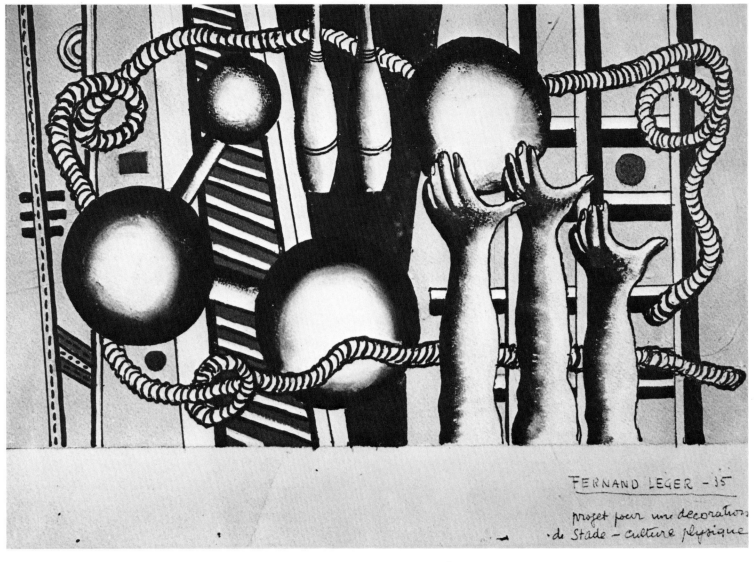

Handwritten on image: FERNAND LEGER - 35
projet pour une décoration
de Stade - culture physique

35. Project for a decoration of a gymnasium. 1935. Gouache, 6 3/4 × 11 3/4″. Private collection

subject to the overriding laws of the picture even when they are entrusted with the burden of the statement. However greatly it might vary, the artist had found his idiom once and for all and could venture on the "grand subject" without the slightest risk of going astray.

The figures in the monumental compositions of 1935–39 are gymnasts, acrobats, and artistes. They are not depicted in full action but face the spectator with graceful gestures that recall the finale of an acrobatic turn. They show no trace of the popular directness of *Three Musicians* (colorplate 33). But, compared with the figures of the early twenties, they seem more relaxed: their forms are rounder, their limbs more agile, their faces a degree more natural. They are a unique combination of the ideal and the real, of solemnity and triteness. Their still-stereotyped features and the affected gestures that contrast oddly with their colossal

frames make them denizens of an ideal sphere; but their sturdy physique and the trite insignia of their calling—tights, tattooings, and paraphernalia—anchor them to reality. In the props that accompany them—emblems rather than the tools of their trade—the almost photographic precision of the still lifes Léger painted about 1925 has all but disappeared; now they are scattered like highly decorative materials, representational or abstract, over the huge canvas. Ideality, standardization, and festiveness as displayed in these works are the conditions demanded by murals in the grand style, and it was consistent with this manner that Léger accepted monumental commissions. In 1935 he designed murals for the French pavilion at the Brussels World's Fair; in 1937 he did a monumental painting, *Le Transport des forces*, for the Palais de la Découverte in Paris.

During the thirties Léger painted a great many

34

still lifes. They reveal the same change in style as his large compositions—free-floating forms, often abstract or floral; plantlike instead of geometric forms, which become increasingly rare. It is significant that Léger busied himself just then more intensively with drawings from nature: leaves, roots, and tree trunks. Plant life, which first appeared with a new freedom in *Woman Bathing* of 1931 (colorplate 28), assumes an importance in his work that his "Mechanical Period" would hardly have led one to expect. Culminating points in the long line of still lifes are pictures like *Butterfly and Flower* and *Still Life on a Blue Ground*, both of 1937.

There is no specifically American period in Léger's artistic development. His art evolved slowly from its own premises. But there was an American phenomenon that made an impact on his art: Times Square at night, with the flashing lights of the advertisements throwing constantly changing colors on the scene. That experience led him to employ stripes and patches of color more freely and independently of the design. Léger applied this principle of free-colored forms in a large number of his works, including the definitive versions of *The Country Outing* (colorplate 39) and *The Great Parade* (colorplate 40), but it did not dominate his late period and remained merely one of his many methods of color articulation. Another American experience was that of "bad taste," which, if it did not influence him, at least confirmed him in his chosen path. In other respects America did not change either Léger's style or his subject matter. He was almost sixty years old when he settled there, and he no longer needed external stimuli. Indeed,

36. POLYCHROME FLOWER. 1936. Oil on canvas, 35 × 51″. Galerie Louise Leiris, Paris

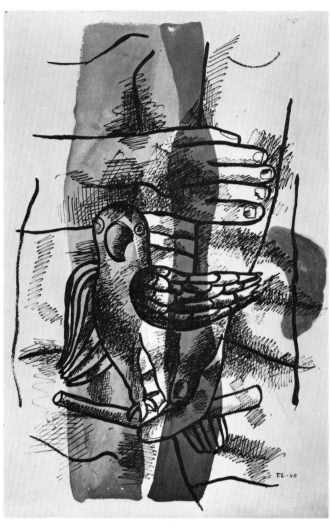

37. THE PARROT. 1940. Gouache and India ink,
17 3/8 × 11 3/4". Private collection, Paris

colorplate 37, figs. 42, 43); the Country Outing series of 1943–54 (see colorplate 39, fig. 45); and lastly *The Great Parade*, which began with a charcoal drawing in 1940 and culminated in the definitive version of 1954 (colorplate 40). That Léger was destined to be a great mural painter becomes increasingly evident. In fact, he received more and more monumental commissions, including the mosaic for the façade of the church at Assy, the stained-glass windows for the churches of Audincourt and Courfaivre (Switzerland), the murals for the large hall of the United Nations building in New York, and the window for the University of Caracas.

In the many-figured compositions of his late period, Léger's art assumes the character of an epic pictorial world as simple as it is exuberant. He scatters figures and objects about with incredible prodigality. He tells us of divers in the port of Marseilles, construction workers on building sites, excursionists on weekend outings, acrobats in the circus. The austere, ideal spirit that imbues his pictures of the thirties is now replaced by a smiling gaiety whose exuberance is held in check only by the honest use of the medium. No longer content to display objects and figures, Léger now tells us about them. And he does so almost after the man-

surveying the works he produced between 1940 and 1945, one cannot discover in them the slightest trace of the catastrophe of World War II.

Léger's will to monumentality was amazingly intensified in the works executed during the last fifteen years of his life, when he concentrated his artistic effort on large compositions. The major works and final versions are not the only ones that count; they are surrounded by a quantity of pictures in which the various elements of the composition appear isolated or grouped. The big pictures of acrobats produced in the thirties were already a sort of cycle, for, as mentioned before, Léger always tended to employ a motif or a form in different contexts. In the same way, the groups of works of his late period also expanded to form large cycles, such as the Divers of 1941–45 (see colorplate 32, fig. 39); the Girls on Bicycles series (see colorplate 38, fig. 41) that started in 1943 and ended in the big *Homage to Louis David* (colorplate 36); the Constructors of 1949–51 (see

38. THE DANCE. 1942. Oil on canvas, 72 × 60 3/4".
Galerie Louise Leiris, Paris

39. THE DIVERS. 1945. Oil on canvas, 76 3/4 × 57 1/2″. Städtische Kunsthalle, Mannheim

40. COMPOSITION FOR A MURAL PAINTING. 1950. Oil on canvas, 23 3/4 × 36 1/4″. Private collection

ner of the strip cartoon, using simple themes, simple lines, simple colors, and action that can be understood at a glance. In these works he achieves a naiveté of handling and expression that strikes one as the happy reward of his lifelong effort toward simplicity, a naiveté that combines extreme artistic maturity with the spirit of monumental art.

The people depicted in these works seem to have neither troubles nor problems—in a word, they seem to be happy. But when we peer into their faces we miss any trace of joy: there is no room for emotion of any sort. Joy is expressed in the artistic handling, as well as in the subject matter—women on their cycles, vacationers at their picnics, artistes in their studied postures, even construction workers under the blue sky, looking more like gymnasts than working men. With the exception of these latter, in his last great cycles Léger celebrated not so much work as freedom from work—leisure, enjoyment, relaxation. True, this relaxation is the corollary of work, for obviously the heroes of these pictures belong to the "working" class and therefore to the same working world

that Léger took as the basic theme of his "Mechanical Period." Extolling as they do the liberty, fraternity, and equality of the working people, these pictures in their totality are a grand apotheosis of liberty. Léger has raised a monument to the reality of the people and to the ideal of liberty—real and ideal in one. Man's age-old dream of an earthly paradise is linked with the reality of the class to which Léger declared his social and political allegiance during those years. He became the prophet of a dreamed-of reality of free, equal, fraternal men and women, which he situated not in a distant Tahiti but in a possible future that was worth fighting—and painting—for. Gauguin's utopianism is set in a new mold together with the nineteenth century's faith in progress, which Gauguin had expressed only with "contrary signs." Léger, too, believed in the possibility of a better world.

In Picasso—to refer once again to Léger's great antipode—there is no trace or echo of this "realistic idealism," except perhaps in the works of the Antibes series of 1946, for they, too, are the apotheosis of a state of celestial bliss. But instead of simple people, they are inhabited by fauns and centaurs—the mythological paraphrase of a heavenly moment in the painter's life. Whatever aspect it assumes, Picasso's art is always autobiographical, and for that very reason it assumes countless new disguises. Léger's art shows no trace of this autobiographical character: his center of gravity is shifted from within to without, from the subject of the artist to the objectivity of form and color, of man and object, of space and time. Even in his idealistic compositions Léger never turns his back on the real world, and it is in this world that he wants not only to paint but also to act. Thus for him the collective commissions he received in greater numbers

after 1945—murals, stained-glass windows, mosaics, tapestries—were the fulfillment of an ardent desire and not, as for Picasso, merely other dimensions of his own activity.

Léger's late works—and this is also true, up to a point, of the pictures he painted in the twenties—brought him into close contact with a generation that did not begin to make its voice heard until many years after his death. This generation loved the blunt directness and shrill colors of commercial art, the trivial products of the consumer-goods industry; it instinctively shunned what is cultivated, differentiated, modulated. To Kandinsky's dogma of the "intellectual in art" it opposed a concept which, though seemingly utterly anti-intellec-

41. FOUR GIRLS ON BICYCLES. 1943–48. Oil on canvas, 51 × 63 3/4″. Musée National Fernand Léger, Biot

42. CONSTRUCTORS ON A BLUE BACKGROUND. 1950. Gouache, 20 1/8 × 26 3/8″. Private collection, Paris

left: 43. THE CONSTRUCTORS. 1950.
Oil on canvas, 38 1/8 × 51″.
Collection Louis Clayeux, Paris

44. THE TWO LOVERS. 1953. Heightened drawing,
25 3/4 × 19 1/2". Private collection

tual, revealed its spirit in its ruthless negation of spirituality. The more contemporary this generation was, the more modern it felt itself to be. America set its stamp upon it, and Léger may have been more indebted to America than he himself believed for the uninhibited directness of color, form, and figure in his late compositions. One must, as he said, be in harmony with one's generation. And he not only painted in harmony with his own generation, but extended that harmony far beyond it at an age when he would have been justified in seeking refuge in an elderly style. Léger could never have imagined how closely the young would follow in his footsteps. Though he did not make the slightest effort to keep up to date, the development of his art during the last fifteen years of his life represents an amazing process of artistic rejuvenation. And it was due not only to the undiminished vitality of his painterly temperament but also to the undoubted topicality of his painting, its modernity, and its permanence long after his death. Léger,

particularly in his last phase, has proved to be one of the most stable bridges between the pioneers of twentieth-century art, who were his contemporaries, and the artists of the younger generation.

Léger's work stands foursquare, broad-based, space-filling, and colorful amid the art of the first half of the twentieth century—a really monumental body of work, but monumental not so much in its actual dimensions and execution as in its style and spirit, its tendency to largeness, its *will* to monumentality. If one tries to imagine the art of our century without this mighty presence, one realizes how much Léger enriched it through the fullness of his creations; indeed, through the fullness of each individual picture. For sensuous fullness, an essential feature of modern art, is more strongly marked in Fernand Léger than in any other painter—more so, especially, than in those painters who, like him, had ideas about changing the world. Full-bodied colors and forms, full-bodied figures and objects, these meant more to him than the spirituality extolled by others. He was concerned not with the finer mental or spiritual values but with almost physical values: with the power and reality of colors and forms, with the physical presence of human figures. Léger never set out to plumb the depths of the human soul nor to scale the heights of the human spirit. On the picture as such he conferred a sturdy, trustworthy reality of its own. Thus conceived, colors and forms were to him quite as real as men and things, and vice versa; men and things were real for him only when represented in terms of the present—which for him meant: when they submitted to the primacy of color and form. He kept to this basic conception even in the case of his motors and machinery, which he glorified as representing the spirit of the age. And that he did not sacrifice his aesthetic credo even to them shows that Léger was both a contemporary and a painter, in the full sense of both words.

He had an unshakable confidence in the aesthetic that he professed, an aesthetic which transcended "art for art's sake" and amounted to a moral conception of art's place in the contemporary world. His self-confidence is manifested not only by his steady output of pictures but also by the lectures and writings in which he set forth his deepest convictions, again and again, with unflagging emphasis. Léger never allowed himself to be lured away by side issues or nice distinctions. Such distinctions seemed to him merely a matter of taste, which did not correspond to his own and might even be contrary to it; but he regarded them "objectively" as being indicative of a definite social class, the "ruling" class, and irrelevant to our time. He was not disposed to flatter "bourgeois" taste, as did so much proletarian art; and he accepted the fact that many art lovers who admired contemporaries like Picasso and Braque did not find his work appealing. On the one hand, Léger was anxious to reach the public through his art; not for him the "splendid isolation" of the artist. On the other, his own style forced him into isolation. Unlike Picasso, who, living on the fringe of society, was a law unto himself and was thus accepted by society as a brilliant outsider, Léger wished to bring about social changes, or at least to sanction them through his art. He regarded "modern" society as his secret patron and himself as the man best qualified to carry out its commissions. That is to say, he supplied good, solid painting on readily understandable themes that raised no problems and called for no heart-searching; but he presented a kind of *imagerie populaire* of his time which, however —and this was his tragedy—never had much chance of becoming popular. Aiming above all, as he repeatedly declared, at an objective and unsentimental art designed to satisfy an anonymous, collective society, he found himself opposed and thwarted by the latent demand of that society for subjective and sentimental values, such as the cinema affords. Léger wished to make simple pictures for simple people unprivileged by birth and education; but his pictures ended up in "bourgeois" collections, whether public or private.

45. THE COUNTRY OUTING. 1954. Oil on canvas, 76 1/2 × 76 1/2".
Private collection. Courtesy of Madeleine Chalette-Lejwa

He was a socialist realist, a socialist utopian. But his work has little to do with the official Soviet ideology. He refused to sacrifice the free use of his artistic means, the autonomy of color and form, to social purposes. For him there was no turning back to naturalism, not even in his Constructors, though the pictures on this theme show a slight tendency in this direction. It was his rooted conviction that the artist's commitment to the present requires him to employ the means of expression of his own time.

For all his passionate repudiation of everything subjective and his passionate pursuit of objectivity, Léger never ceased to speak out in his own superbly personal language. The will to objectivity called for the whole subjective strength of his being. Yet, in the end, spiritual and artistic vitality is revealed as the great virtue of his art. His pictures do not *tell* us about Léger, they *are* Léger. This was not the self-absorption of a Picasso; but the age of artistic individualism was by no means brought to an end by Léger. If during his lifetime and long afterward he was a figure of some notoriety, this was due to his objective and rational outlook, his obvious concern with commonplace things, his eager acceptance of modern realities, his stated faith in a better future for mankind. Still, as an artist whose art owes its caliber to the caliber of its maker's personality and derives its grandeur from that anything-but-anonymous or collective quality, he takes his place in the "classic" generation of early-twentieth-century artists and, indeed, in the rich tradition of middle-class painting, which owes its luster to so many great artists and which, in Léger's generation, reached a new, perhaps final climax.

46. THE PARADE. 1954. Gouache, 19 1/4 × 21 1/4". Private collection, Paris

47. THE CHILDREN'S GARDEN. Polychrome sculpture. Musée National Fernand Léger, Biot

48. Façade of the Musée National Fernand Léger at Biot

BIOGRAPHICAL OUTLINE

The information given here is largely based on the biography in the catalogue of the Fernand Léger exhibition at the Grand Palais, Paris, October 1971–January 1972.

49. Fernand Léger with Picasso, André Verdet, and Nadia at Picasso's house at Vallauris

1881   Born on February 4 at Argentan, Normandy.

1890–96   Attends school at Argentan and Tinchebray.

1897–99   Apprenticeship with an architect in Caen.

1900–02   Works as a draftsman in an architect's office in Paris.

1902–3   Military service at Versailles.

1903   Attends classes at the École des Arts Décoratifs, Paris. Free student at the École des Beaux-Arts. Attends the Académie Julian.

1904   Works in an architect's office, and does retouching for a photographer.

1905–6   Illness. Spends the winter at Belgodère in Corsica.

1907   Cézanne retrospective exhibition at the Salon d'Automne, Paris.

1908–9   Several visits to Corsica. Studio in "La Ruche" (Montparnasse). Becomes friendly with Delaunay, Chagall, Soutine, Archipenko, Laurens, Lipchitz, Apollinaire, Max Jacob, Reverdy, Blaise Cendrars, Maurice Raynal.

1909   Meets the Douanier Rousseau.

1910   With Jacques Villon, Delaunay, Le Fauconnier, Gleizes, André Mare, Picabia, Kupka, and Marie Laurencin, takes part in the meetings that lead to the founding of the Section d'Or group (1912).

1911   Exhibits his *Nudes in the Forest* at the Salon des Indépendants.

1912   Exhibits at the Galerie Kahnweiler, Paris.

1913   Signs an exclusive contract with D.-H. Kahnweiler. Gives a lecture at the Wassilew Academy, Berlin, "The Origins of Painting and its Representative Value."

1914   Lecture at the Wassilew Academy, Berlin, "Present-Day Achievements in Painting."

1914–16   Serves in the French army.

1916   Gassed on the Verdun front.

1917   Hospitalized at Villepinte in the suburbs of Paris and discharged from the army at the end of the year.

1918   Illustrations for *J'ai tué* by Blaise Cendrars.

1919   Marries Jeanne Lohy. Illustrations for *La Fin du monde filmée par l'ange Notre-Dame* by Blaise Cendrars. Exhibits at the gallery L'Effort Moderne (Léonce Rosenberg), Paris.

1920   Gallery and magazine *L'Esprit nouveau* founded by Ozenfant and Le Corbusier. Meets Le Corbusier.

1921   Works with Blaise Cendrars on the film *La Roue* produced by Abel Gance. First contacts with Mondrian and Theo van Doesburg.

Illustrations for *Lunes en papier* by André Malraux.

1922 Designs the curtain, sets, and costumes for the Swedish ballet *Skating Rink* by Rolf de Maré (music by Arthur Honegger).

1923 Sets and costumes for the ballet *La Création du monde* (music by Darius Milhaud, scenario by Blaise Cendrars). Sets and costumes for the film *L'Inhumaine* by Marcel L'Herbier.

1924 Opens a free studio with Ozenfant, where he teaches with Marie Laurencin and Alexandra Exter. Produces the film *Ballet mécanique* (photography by Man Ray and Dudley Murphy, music by George Antheil). Journey to Italy with Léonce Rosenberg. Lecture at the Sorbonne, "Le Spectacle."

1925 At the Salon des Arts Décoratifs, Paris, Léger and Delaunay decorate the entrance hall of the "French Embassy" pavilion (architect Robert Mallet-Stevens). First murals for the "Esprit Nouveau" pavilion (architect Le Corbusier). First exhibition in the United States (Anderson Galleries, New York).

1928 Trip to Berlin for the opening of his one-man show at the Flechtheim Gallery. Gives a lecture in Berlin on Le Corbusier.

1929 Teaches at the Académie Moderne with Ozenfant.

1931 First visit to the United States (New York and Chicago).

1932 Teaches at the Académie de la Grande-Chaumière, Paris. Trip to Sweden and Norway.

1933 Trip to Zurich for his exhibition at the Kunsthaus. Trip to Greece with Le Corbusier.

1934 Trip to London. Sets for the Alexander Korda film *The Shape of Things to Come*, based on the book by H. G. Wells. Lecture at the Sorbonne, "From the Acropolis to the Eiffel Tower." Trip to Stockholm.

1935 Murals for a hall at the Brussels World's Fair. Second trip to the United States, with Le Corbusier. Exhibits at the Art Institute of Chicago and The Museum of Modern Art, New York.

1936 Takes part in the debate "The Quarrel over Realism" at the Maison de la Culture, Paris, with Aragon and Le Corbusier.

1937 Sets for the Serge Lifar ballet *David triomphant* at the Paris Opéra. Scenery for the Trade Union Festival at the Vélodrome d'Hiver and mural (*Le Transport des forces*) for the Palais de la Découverte.

1938 Third trip to the United States. Decorates the New York apartment of Nelson A. Rockefeller. Stays in Provincetown with John Dos Passos and on Long Island with the architect W. K. Harrison. Gives a course of eight lectures at Yale, "Color in Architecture."

1939 Sets for Jean-Richard Bloch's play *La Naissance d'une cité* (music by Darius Milhaud and Arthur Honegger), performed at the Vélodrome d'Hiver, Paris.

1940 Sails for the United States in October. Teaches at Yale University.

1941 Teaches at Mills College, Oakland, California. At the Pierre Matisse Gallery in New York, meets the exiled artists Masson, Tanguy, Matta, Breton, Zadkine, Ernst, Chagall, Mondrian, and Ozenfant.

1944 Composes the sequence *La Fille au coeur fabrique* for Hans Richter's film *Dreams That Money Can Buy*. Exhibits in New York, Chicago, and Cincinnati.

1945 Exhibits in Cambridge. Returns to France in December. Joins the French Communist party.

1946 First exhibition at the Galerie Louis Carré, Paris.

1946–49 Façade mosaic for the church at Assy (Haute-Savoie).

1948 Sets for the ballet *Le Pas d'acier* (music by Prokofiev) for the Ballet des Champs-Élysées. Takes part in the Peace Congress at Wroclaw (Breslau), Poland. Joint lecture with Jean Bazaine in Brussels, "The Art of Today."

1949 Text and illustrations for *Le Cirque*. Illustrations for Rimbaud's *Illuminations*. Sets and costumes for Darius Milhaud's *Bolivar* at the Paris Opéra. Does his first ceramics, at Biot (Alpes-Maritimes). Retrospective exhibition at the Musée National d'Art Moderne, Paris. Traveling exhibition in Freiburg im Breisgau, Hamburg, Basel, and Hanover.

1950 Death of Jeanne Léger. Sets up a ceramics workshop at Biot. Mosaic for the crypt of the American Memorial at Bastogne, Belgium. Exhibition at the Tate Gallery, London.

1951 Designs stained-glass windows for the church at Audincourt (Doubs). Decoration for the French pavilion at the Milan Triennale. *The Constructors* exhibited at the Maison de la Pensée Française, Paris.

1952 Marries Nadia Khodossevitch, his pupil since 1924 and his studio assistant. Settles at Gif-sur-Yvette (Seine-et-Oise). Murals for the United Nations Building in New York. Sets and costumes for a Janine Charrat ballet performed at Amboise for the 500th anniversary of the birth of Leonardo da Vinci. Exhibition at the Kunsthalle, Bern.

1953 Illustrations for Paul Éluard's poem *Liberté*. Exhibition at the Art Institute of Chicago.

1954 Designs windows for the church at Courfaivre, Switzerland, and for the University of Caracas, Venezuela. Exhibition at the Maison de la Pensée Française, Paris.

1955 Awarded the Grand Prize at the São Paulo Bienal. Sculpture, ceramic, and mosaic for the Gaz de France coking plant at Alfortville, in the Paris suburbs. Retrospective exhibition at the Lyons Museum. Attends the Sokol Congress in Prague. Dies at Gif-sur-Yvette on August 17.

COLORPLATES

NUDES IN THE FOREST

Painted 1909–10. Oil on canvas, 47 1/4 × 67"
Kröller-Müller State Museum, Otterlo

At first glance a compact, chaotic congeries of cylindrical forms in tonal colors. By degrees three huge naked figures emerge from the rubble-like mass and the few vertical lines of the picture—one kneeling frontally on the left; a second seated in the middle; a third, viewed from the back, standing on the right. The broken verticals turn out to be trees and the whole scene a section of forest with woodcutters. The ground is strewn with chunks of wood and a scattering of green plants here and there.

This monumental painting was Fernand Léger's first contribution to the history of contemporary art. It marked his definitive break with the Impressionist tradition he had till then adhered to and his immediate entry into the discussion of a new concept of what constitutes a picture. *Nudes in the Forest* is one of the outstanding works by which a new generation of artists freed itself from the fetters of the past. When it was exhibited at the memorable Salon des Indépendants of 1911 it created a huge sensation.

Four years earlier, the great memorial show of Cézanne's work that made a decisive impact on all future art had been held in the Salon d'Automne. "I sometimes ask myself," Léger said later, "what contemporary painting would be like without Cézanne. . . . Cézanne taught me to love forms and volumes; he made me concentrate on drawing. It was then that I felt that drawing must be strict and absolutely unsentimental." In *Nudes in the Forest* Léger applied almost literally Cézanne's theory that nature is built up of the elementary stereometric forms—sphere, cone, and cylinder—and, indeed, went far beyond Cézanne himself in this respect. He smashed to pieces and radically destroyed the organic continuum of nature, depicting it as a primeval, earthquake-shattered, rocky landscape inhabited, fittingly enough, by a race of primitive giants. Cubism has often been mistaken for a movement that laid form in ruins; here the ruins are piled up all around us, but they are the ruins of objects—mangled trunks and branches—and serve as elements of a new concept of form.

The destruction of nature's organic continuum and its restructuring out of stereometric formal elements—that is the real theme of the picture, which overshadows the apparent theme of the woodcutters in the forest. This brought Léger close to Cubism, which at that time was going though its "analytical" phase—in which nature was analyzed with an eye to its possibilities for Cubist interpretation. Actually, the language of Léger's Cubism—massive, violent, compact—differs from that of Picasso and Braque. Every form is endowed with the maximum of solid volume. The trees are like pipes, discontinuous in shape and color. A few years earlier the Fauves had been fond of stressing the autonomy of color by painting tree trunks in sections of various hues; here Léger stresses the autonomy of form by building up his trees of angular sections. With this "brutal" method of destroying the organic continuum, he achieved a furious dynamism of spaces and volumes that calls to mind Futurism rather than Cubism. Every form seems hewn with an ax from the raw material of nature. Even through the human figures there flows no coherent vital lymph: they act abruptly, like robots; each limb is an independent form; the hands with fingers bent to grip space resemble steel gauntlets; even the hair seems chiseled into hard, sculptural forms. To use Léger's own words, "For me *Nudes in the Forest* was a battle of volumes."

The splendid nudes drawn during the previous years, at once sketchy and sculptural, show us how Léger came to construct his figures in this way. At that time Negro sculpture was all the rage and greatly prized by artists. There is little doubt that it influenced the antiorganic structural principle on which these statuesque figures are based. But there is no sign of any external kinship, such as existed in Picasso's "Negro Period." Just then Léger was strongly attracted to Alexandèr Archipenko's sculptures but not directly influenced by them. His woodcutters seem somewhat to anticipate Duchamp-Villon's curious *Horse* of 1914, which occupies a place of its own in the sculpture of that day. Similarly, Duchamp-Villon's *Torso of a Young Man* (1910) is closer to the figures of Léger's early masterpiece than any other contemporary work. That Léger had not yet come in contact with Picasso's art when he did *Nudes in the Forest* is clearly demonstrated by the great differences in style. There is a certain resemblance to Picasso's *Nude in the Forest* of 1908 (now in Moscow) with its heavy, massive limbs; but it is quite plausible that comparable forms of this sort derived independently from Cézanne.

The spectacle this painting offers us is first of all pictorial. But whereas Picasso and Braque experimented with their new techniques in landscapes, still lifes, and portraits, Léger took work as his theme. The men he painted were no mere models but emphatically workers, and the theme he tackled here for the first time occupied him all his life, right up to *The Constructors* of 1950 (colorplate 37). The subject was an "alibi" for pictorial procedures; it was an essential part of his creed. And that creed, together with the "grand style," gives the workers in his forest picture a certain heroic character that is all the more noticeable because in this early phase of his art Léger had not yet completely abandoned genre painting. Similarly, the light still possesses an illustrative, romantic character because its function had not yet been delegated to "pure," bright colors.

THE WEDDING

Painted 1910–11. Oil on canvas, 101 × 81 1/8''
Musée National d'Art Moderne, Paris

During the years 1911 and 1912 Léger approached very close to Cubism while distinguishing himself by his own personal version of it. By this time Cubism had reached a phase in which objects and figures were no longer forced to assume crystalline forms and the rhythm of lines and planes was liberated from all trace of representation. A picture was viewed as an autonomous graphic-painterly organism whose structure combined barely recognizable remnants of objects and figures fused in a free rhythm. The picture is all; the object, where still recognizable, is nothing.

Léger resisted the temptation of this new type of painting except insofar as it was compatible with his strong pictorial will. This is clearly seen in the big *Wedding* of 1910–11, where the vertical composition and the fragmentary rhythm of the forms directly recall the works Picasso and Braque produced in that same year. But it differs from the works of the classic Cubists in that individual shapes emerge formally or in color from the dense Cubist fabric. This is the starting point of a trend to elementary forms—with a bias toward geometry—and colors. The homogeneous structure of Cubist painting is broken up by a more contrasted language: large areas vie with small, colored with uncolored, dark with light, planes with volumes, straight lines with curves. One understands that Léger—like Delaunay, who coined the term—saw the pictures of Picasso and Braque as "spider webs" and opposed their delicate, lyrical constructions with his harsher accents.

The text of the picture is not easy to read. The fragments of figures, houses, and trees are quite recognizable, but they hardly add up to a "wedding." The figures have lost the preponderance they had in *Nudes in the Forest* (colorplate 1) and have not yet regained it, as they did in Léger's later works. But it is significant that even here, however small and fragmented they may seem, they are more important than in the pictures produced by the Cubists of Montmartre at that time. Cascades of small cylindrical forms rise confusedly one above the other in two vertical zones. Whereas in Picasso and Braque the individual forms are structured in a flat painterly fashion and embedded in the general composition, here each bodily form has its own stereometric volume, quite distinct from the flat areas nearby. This destroys the unity of space and recreates it piecemeal. The very lack of space in the tightly packed figures points to space. Space—absolutely without perspective, in contrast to *Nudes in the Forest*—is created under the surging movements of the masses and only secondarily through the relationship of the figures in the foreground to the minute houses in the distance. It develops dynamically before our eyes and this dynamism, too, is more akin to Futurism than to Cubism.

Léger's closest friend at that time was Robert Delaunay, four years his junior, to whom the spreading influence of Cubism owed more, perhaps, than to the Cubists themselves. Delaunay's painting was going through its Eiffel Tower phase, between the pictures of the Church of Saint-Séverin and his pure-colored "Orphism." But from 1910 to 1912 he also produced his monumental picture *City of Paris*, many aspects of which recall Léger. The latter's *Wedding* reminds one of Delaunay by its dynamic verticality; its lively spaciousness; the cleavage of space by large, bright, sharply defined areas that enter the picture plane from the side; the trend toward elementary geometric forms; and most of all, the combination of Cubist structure with independent color.

THE SMOKERS

Painted 1911. Oil on canvas, 51 × 37 7/8"
The Solomon R. Guggenheim Museum, New York City

The progression from *The Wedding* (colorplate 2) through *The Smokers* to *Woman in Blue* (colorplate 4) demonstrates with the utmost clarity how logically Léger's art developed in 1911 and 1912, the years of his truly Cubist period. All the features one observes in *The Wedding* appear considerably intensified in the pictures he painted next, and his insistence on style in the midst of Cubist forms is even clearer and more resolute.

That Léger found pleasure in the theme of a man smoking—not only here but also later—may seem surprising, since the diffuse, nebulous aspect of smoke is inconsistent with his hankering after solid volumes. But perhaps he found stimulation in this very contradiction. By fixing volatile smoke in solid forms he stated his artistic intention still more lucidly. In his *Smokers* the clouds of smoke are not airy vapors but impenetrable shapes composed of stereometric elements.

There is no difficulty in defining the scene: men smoking pipes before a hilly landscape on the outskirts of the city; by their side, a table with a dish full of pears; a street lined with houses and trees climbing the hill in the background. A hanging piece of violet cloth in the top left-hand corner indicates that we are in a dwelling, perhaps on a balcony. A decoration of this kind was quite alien to the Cubism of Picasso and Braque. From a distance, partly, no doubt, because of the general style and the painterly handling, *The Smokers* calls to mind pictures Chagall produced at that time, such as the large *I and the Village* of 1911–12 with its faces in the foreground and dream houses in the distance. Needless to say, Léger had no use for dreams; what he aimed at was quite simply a picture composed in accordance with his own laws.

The steeply rising clouds of smoke repeat the pale vertical sections of *The Wedding* in a simplified, more clearly defined stereometry. The staccato rhythm of the small forms amid the larger ones is also clarified and relaxed. The swarming confusion of *The Wedding* has become an assemblage of figures and objects. The color is given greater prominence. And the representational element is more strongly stressed, as if the artist no longer shrank from recognizing that things like trees and houses are entitled to a more important place in the picture.

It is quite in keeping with the artistic development of Léger's generation that material things achieve the rank of pictorial values, speak the language of the picture, be governed by pictorial laws, and, in order to perform their function in the picture, that their forms undergo modification and disruption. But Léger added a new, seemingly contradictory contribution of his own. Not content with giving material things a formal quality, he wanted equally to give forms a material quality. This material quality consists not in the recognizability of the forms as objects but in their corporeal substantiality. A cloud of smoke does not have to look like smoke, but it cannot be a mere abstract form—it must have the quality of an object. A treetop does not have to be treelike; it has to be like an object. In this picture one comes repeatedly up against the hard corners of objects, although the artist was not greatly interested in realistic portrayal. What held his attention was not the branches and leaves of the trees but their elemental forms, their volumes, and their quality as "objects." Object and form achieve a new identity that has nothing to do with naturalism. This is the basis of Léger's art.

For the sake of this "objectivity" Léger sees no difference between human figures and inanimate objects. In the picture the human figures are treated like objects of a different formal constitution from, but of the same substance as, the other objects in the picture. The human figures in *Nudes in the Forest* (colorplate 1) are still mythical athletes; the smokers are "uninteresting" as humans. Their significance lies in their form and in their assimilation to the other objects in the picture. For this reason they are not entrusted with a special "statement." The statement is distributed over the whole picture; the "expressive" or "sentimental" concentration on the human figures and faces is banned.

That the color contrasts are stronger in *The Smokers* than in *The Wedding* can be seen at a glance; indeed, by comparison the latter picture seems almost monochrome. This is due no doubt to the greater range of colors in *The Smokers*, but more especially it is owing to Léger's permanent obsession with the law of contrasts. "Pictorial contrasts," he wrote in 1913, "have become the backbone of modern painting." And in 1914 he formulated his thinking in words that sound like a commentary on *The Smokers*:

Contrasts = dissonances. Let us take as an example any subject you like—for instance, the visual effect of the curling, rounded clouds of smoke that rise among houses and whose plastic value you want to render. . . . Concentrate your curves with the greatest possible variety but do not separate them; frame them with the hard, dry rapport of the house walls—dead surfaces that achieve mobility because their colors contrast with the central mass and they are opposed to living forms. You will obtain the maximum effect.

WOMAN IN BLUE

Painted 1912. Oil on canvas, 76 3/8 × 51''
Kunstmuseum, Basel

"A picture," said Léger, "is based on harmonious relationships between volumes, lines, and colors. These are the three forces that must govern a work of art. If, when harmonizing these three essential elements, it happens that objects—namely, elements of reality—can be inserted in the composition, that may perhaps be better and result in an enrichment. But they are subordinated to the three basic elements mentioned above." And in another context: "A picture organized and orchestrated like a musical score, the absolute geometrical requirements . . . the weight of the volumes, the relations of the lines, the balance of the colors. All things that demand an absolute order."

Woman in Blue is a thoroughly organized and orchestrated picture. Its "absolute order," rather than its elements—human figures, houses, trees—commands our attention. The colored planes, the large volumes, and the small forms, both flat and round, are distributed over the surface of the picture with a beautiful rhythm. A complex system of black lines provides the scaffolding of the picture. A few large geometric forms, in which curves contrast with straight lines and segments of circles with rectangles in a masterly fashion, supply the basis for an elementary yet differentiated color scheme. For the first time, utterly abstract, "absolute" black appears as the color of large and small planes.

Although this picture is based on absolute order, it has a representational motif—a woman in a blue dress. She is seated on a chair whose back irresistibly calls to mind Brancusi's *Endless Column* of 1918. So much so that one cannot help thinking that Léger exerted a direct influence on the sculptor whose works were so often exhibited side by side with his. The woman is viewed in right profile. Her head can be recognized at the top of the canvas, and the cylindrical forms of her neck and shoulders are even more clearly discernible. Her gauntlet-like hands are folded in her lap. To the right is a table on which stands a decorated cup. To attempt to make out the female figure amid the interplay of abstract forms risks turning the picture into a puzzle. The colored planes overlie the representation quite "regardless," though some have a representational reference. For instance, the blue plane represents the woman's dress; the pale segment of a circle at the bottom of the picture may be her bent knee. There is hardly any other painting of those years in which Léger so strongly emphasized form over figure and object. It is almost "abstract."

For Léger color was what counted most. It was not enough that the Fauves had preached the gospel of pure colors; he had to master it for himself. He took the first step toward that goal in the pictures of 1911, when color became the dominant factor. Léger was in constant communication with his friend Robert Delaunay, who had taken as his mission to combine form freed from the object with color freed from the object. In his *Simultaneous Windows*—a cycle started in 1912—Delaunay broke away from the object almost completely. For him the only real "object" was light, which he celebrated exclusively by means of colors applied on geometrical planes. Delaunay's discoveries in the domain of color had an important influence on Léger, though the artistic aims of the two painters were very different. It was not merely that Léger found little help in Delaunay's theoretical researches; unlike his friend, he wanted to give his colors a maximum of force and therefore a clear, elementary, unequivocal quality. Many years later he recalled, "For me color was an indispensable tonic. In that respect, too, Delaunay and I were poles apart from the rest. They painted in monochrome, we painted in polychrome. After that came the tussle with Delaunay himself. He continued in the wake of the Impressionists by placing two complementary colors, red and green, side by side. I aimed at obtaining tints that isolated themselves, a very red red, a very blue blue. If you set yellow alongside blue, the immediate result is a complementary color, green. So Delaunay tended to nuances, while I sought the total emancipation of color and volume, namely contrast."

Woman in Blue was first painted in a smaller version. Not only does it have a certain sketchlike character; the difference in the upper part is striking. Instead of the large semicircle which in the definitive version is contrapuntal to the circular form at the bottom, there is a trapezoidal plane. Besides that, the female figure is slightly more recognizable as such—a clear proof that in the final version Léger aimed at achieving a high degree of abstraction.

RAILROAD CROSSING

Painted 1912–13. Oil on canvas, 35 7/8 × 31 7/8"
Museum des 20. Jahrhunderts, Vienna

This relaxed landscape is unique in Léger's early work. Compared with his large Cubist compositions, it gives the impression of being serene and unfettered by theoretical intentions. It is neither governed by "absolute order," like *Woman in Blue* (colorplate 4), nor entirely organized down to the very last detail. There are no abstract planes and the scene can be grasped without difficulty. It is as if the artist had taken a day off from the architectural labor of his pictorial constructions and succumbed to the charm of the scenery. As a complete master of his idiom, he can allow himself the luxury of being, for once, more representational. But even as he keeps his eye on the "motif," he produces what is obviously a "Léger."

True, this interest in houses and trees also constituted a turning point: a year or two later he did his village pictures. Léger's love for objects was such that he could not dispense with them for long. Even where insistence on form was strongest, they could not be simply submerged by the form. For this reason *Railroad Crossing* has a place of its own between pictures like *Woman in Blue* and those he painted next.

It is significant that the artist was not satisfied with pure scenery. He preferred an inhabited landscape, and here the gates of the railroad crossing add a (still very low) civilizing tone. Léger's abhorrence of sentimentality led him to avoid nature in the raw, to set up a barrier between it and himself—in the literal sense of the word. In his eyes the five towering bars of the gate make nature more "modern" and therefore more beautiful. "The artist must always be in harmony with his epoch," he wrote in 1913, "and so compensate the natural need for varying impressions." In this respect he agreed with Delaunay: "What brought Delaunay and me together was our love of life and movement. He dissected the Eiffel Tower, I took my subject matter from the streets or wherever I happened to find it. . . .

Trains and automobiles, with their plume of smoke or dust, grab all the dynamism for themselves; the scenery becomes secondary and decorative."

True, in *Railroad Crossing* the scenery—in fact, a townscape—is the dominant element, and the dynamic world of engines is indicated only by the bars. Undoubtedly the bars fascinated the painter by their tricolored verticality, which echoes the particolored, angled tree trunks of *Nudes in the Forest* (colorplate 1). Besides, they cut up the landscape in an arbitrary fashion. Nature is limited to the curving green patches of the grass and trees and the circular form of a cloud in the sky. Rotary motions and rounded forms contrast with the straight lines of the bars and the sharp corners of the houses. This picture, though ostensibly a landscape, is actually a rhythmic structure of lines, planes, and colors.

"I want to ignore [the sentimental] viewpoint all my life long. It is an intolerable burden for anyone engaged in plastic art. It is a narcotic, a negative value like the rhyme in poetry." Yet this picture has a sentimental value—what Léger called *une physionomie de joie.*

The motif of the railroad crossing appears again in a painting of 1914 entitled *The Fourteenth of July* (fig. 11). There, too, the landscape is barred by five steeply upright poles. But everything is coarsened and simplified, and on the picture plane spatial continuity is replaced by a vigorous rhythm of black lines and colored forms. The crossing gates are painted in the three colors of the French flag—blue, white, and red. The Fauves—and Van Gogh before them—had already found pleasure in the gay bunting of the French national holiday. Léger utilized the gates of a railroad crossing to obtain the same effect, and they provided the inspiration for a title that, objectively, had nothing to do with them.

HOUSES UNDER THE TREES

Painted 1913. Oil on canvas, 36 1/4 × 28 3/4"
Private collection, Chicago

After the pause of *Railroad Crossing* (colorplate 5) Léger took a similar theme for this picture. But here he has once again engaged his entire artistic will: the village concerns those who live there; what concerns him is the picture. So he tells no more tales of houses, railroad tracks, or crossings. Description is reduced to the minimum; form and color have the first and the last words. But they, too, are greatly reduced. The forms are limited to a few segments of circles, triangles, and rectangles; the colors, to green, red, blue, yellow, violet, white, and the tint of the unprimed canvas. True, the colors themselves are modulated and therefore model the forms they support. But each color shows itself clearly and unreservedly for what it is. Compared with the big pictures of 1911 and 1912, this one is enormously simplified. The juxtaposition of large geometrical planes and an infinity of minute forms has disappeared entirely; now all the forms come from the same type case. Gone also is the contrast between vividly colored planes and toned-down background; the color has the same quality and the same luminosity throughout. As a result, space is condensed to a narrow relief; it exists only insofar as it is replaced by the solids. The law of flatness is honored but broken in the same breath by the solid volumes of houses and trees. After viewing this picture one discovers that there are distinct traces of perspective in works like *The Smokers* (colorplate 3) and *Woman in Blue* (colorplate 4): space extends toward the rear; objects are shrunk by distance; there is a foreground and a background. Nothing of the sort exists in *Houses Under the Trees*, where the roofs are drawn in perspective for the sake, not of space, but of the three-dimensional solid.

"Color is a vital need. It is an indispensable raw material of life, like water and fire," as Léger said in slightly different ways again and again. And in this picture he has treated his colors elementally, like water and fire, like "raw materials." In comparison, *Woman in Blue*, with its more amply differentiated forms and colors, seems "cultivated." Here he has laid his colors on the coarse-grained canvas without a thought to the traditions of French painting. It is as if he combined the colors of the Fauves—André Derain said the tubes of paint must be handled like cartridges of dynamite—with a primitive form of Cubism. Léger brutalized art, not in the sense of brutality, as has often been mistakenly said, but in the sense of Jean Dubuffet's *art brut*. Every element—forms, colors, contrasts, the pulsating rhythm, and the handling—is imbued with a primeval force. But that force is combined with rhythmic, painterly subtlety. Léger's painterly treatment of the various colored forms is extraordinarily fine. Force does not exclude delicacy, nor delicacy force. Nor does the harsh juxtaposition of colors and forms prevent all the elements from achieving a splendid harmony. For all his love of the crude and primitive, Léger's first objectives were balance, harmony, and beauty. Indeed, "beauty" was a word he never shrank from pronouncing.

"Pictorial beauty is entirely independent of sentimental, descriptive, and imitative values," Léger said. As this picture shows, it does not depend on the qualities typical of a village embedded in trees. It is also entirely independent of the romantic nostalgia with which townsmen are fond of transfiguring rural scenes, as Lyonel Feininger did about that time to the Thuringian villages with their Gothic steeples. For Léger a village was neither a townsman's dream nor a rural reality; it was simply a pretext for a picture—a collection of colored cubic houses surrounded by the conical forms of green trees. Indeed, his total concentration on the pictorial values leaves us uncertain—as does the title of the picture—whether in the last analysis this is a village scene or a townscape.

There is an almost identical version of this picture on a smaller scale in the Folkwang Museum in Essen.

VILLAGE IN THE FOREST

Painted 1913. Oil on canvas, 32 1/4 × 39 1/2"
Sprengel Collection, Hanover

In 1913 Léger was deeply concerned with the theme of houses among trees. He was fascinated by the law of "multiplicative contrasts," to which, he thought, artists had paid too little attention. He used to say that he found war much more normal than peace; though, of course, that statement was not meant to be taken in a military sense. "Contrast," he wrote in 1914, "has always frightened peaceable, satisfied people; they do what they can to eliminate it from their lives and, just as they are disagreeably affected by the dissonance of a poster or anything else, their lives are organized so as to avoid all rough contacts. Those are the last circles for an artist to mix with; they wrap up truth and are afraid." When Léger spoke about contrasts he had in mind an artistic truth that is identical with human truth. "Pure color," he said, "involves absolute truth and honesty. With it one never cheats."

In fact, he cannot cheat with his artistic elements: they are there, clear to see, and signify nothing more than what they are—houses, trees with round or pointed crowns, but first of all forms and colors. That they are applied directly on the coarse brown canvas enhances their "truth value" and at the same time eliminates all scope for spatial illusion, since the canvas support is quite blatantly substituted for the natural space. The handling of the surface has become looser and less compact, but that does not tone down the contrapuntal rhythm. On the contrary, the rhythm is still more clearly defined, for the colors are placed one next to the other, as on a flag, and the white planes enliven the entire picture. Nowhere was Léger closer to the Fauves than in this picture, which is one of a series of village landscapes painted in 1913 and 1914. But he combined the Fauvist dogma of pure colors with Cézanne's taut structure and his theory of spheres, cones, and cylinders. Cylindrical forms reappear alongside the spherical forms of the treetops and the cubic forms of the houses; though they represent trees, they really belong to a mechanical world and have no place in the village except as elements of the language of forms.

The artist's explanation of such a high degree of representational shorthand is significant. He based it on the angle from which modern man views the world.

A landscape through which one travels in an automobile or an express train gains in synthetic significance what it loses in descriptive significance. The doors of the railroad car or the windows of the automobile, together with the speed attained, have altered the customary vision of things. Modern man records a hundred times more impressions than an artist did in the eighteenth century; so much so that our language is full of diminutives and abbreviations. This explains the condensation of the modern picture, its variety, its fragmentation of forms. It is certain that the development of means of locomotion and their speed have influenced the new vision. Superficial people cry: "Anarchy!" when faced with these pictures, because they cannot follow in the artistic sphere the evolution of contemporary life as reflected in them. They think there has been a drastic break in continuity, whereas, on the contrary, painting has never been so realistic and so closely linked with its epoch as it is today. Realistic painting in the best sense of the word is just beginning to exist and will not end so soon.

(BOTTOM)

THE STAIRCASE

Painted 1913. Oil on canvas, 56 3/4 × 46 1/2''
Kunsthaus Zurich

Léger's cylindrical forms reappear, though only marginally, in *Village in the Forest* of 1913 (colorplate 7). In *The Staircase* of the same year they virtually monopolize the composition, together with the steps that also occur, only barely visibly, in the village picture and in Léger's strictly Cubist paintings. Here the whole effect is based on contrast: between the cylindrical limbs and the angular steps and between the three primary colors, red, blue, and yellow, augmented by black and white, on a gray ground. The emphasis is placed on solid volumes at the expense of the picture plane, but the modeling is achieved exclusively by juxtaposing unbroken colors.

What is new in this picture and in similar ones of 1912–14—which include a second staircase in oblong format (fig. 13)—is the mechanical, robot-like structure of the human figures. The destruction of the organic factor leads logically to the mechanical, particularly in a painter fascinated by the world of the machine. The human element, reduced to the minimum in *Woman in Blue* (colorplate 4), comes into its own again, in keeping with the new representational trend we observe in the village pictures. But it is a dehumanized humanity, suits of armor rather than living beings. "I didn't feel the human figure just as an object," Léger said, "but since I found the machine so plastic, I wanted to give the human figure the same plasticity." He could not have expressed his aversion to expressiveness and sentimentality more drastically than by replacing the heads with two lancette-shaped ovals, part black and part white. And instead of the face, the seat of human expression, he has put an inert form. This avoidance of the human countenance with its psychological and individual qualities is typical of works produced by a host of artists before and after 1920. Some avoided it for the sake of poetic or surreal values, others for purely plastic values, replacing it with simple "forms."

In 1912, a year before Léger's *Staircase*, Marcel Duchamp painted his famous *Nude Descending a Staircase*, in which the human figure is reduced to a metal structure that functions like a robot. Here Futurist notions, such as the simultaneity of the successive phases of descent, are combined with the monochromy of Cubism; and the artist has also forgone the human countenance. Duchamp and Léger were very close at that time, but no less significant than the occurrence of similar themes in their pictures is the total discrepancy of their artistic aims. Léger had none of Duchamp's intellectual keenness or experimental curiosity. He painted like a painter. And even when, as here, he allowed his sculptural figures a civilizing trait, he did so—quite unlike Duchamp—in a primitive, solid, uncomplicated, "wholesome" language. Indeed, one of the factors of Léger's greatness is that he fixed the complex world of technology in a formula of insuperable simplicity—and, what is more, a formula that is typically painterly. Always a painter and always simple, he yet succeeded in making his technoid forms suggest the world of the machine, by which, as an artist consciously and enthusiastically of this century, he was irresistibly fascinated.

The great love Léger and Delaunay shared for the technology and tempo of their day was directly derived from Futurism. It was the Futurists who purposively introduced the fascination of technological progress to the arts. In 1909 Marinetti's Futurist Manifesto was published in *Le Figaro*, where Léger and the other French artists could read the following: "We maintain that the glories of the world have been enriched with a new beauty—the beauty inherent in speed. A racing car, its hood embellished with thick pipes that resemble snakes breathing fire . . . an automobile whose roar resembles machine-gun fire, is far more beautiful than the Nike of Samothrace. We want to sing the praises of the man who holds in his hands the steering wheel, whose shaft ideally pierces the earth as it careers frantically round its orbit." And the Manifesto of the Futurist Painters of 1910 says: "Only that art is capable of expression which finds its elements in the environment in which it lives. Our forebears took their subjects from the religious atmosphere that impressed their souls; we must be inspired by the palpable miracles of contemporary life." And that is exactly what Léger did.

CONTRAST OF FORMS

Painted 1914. Oil on canvas, 31 3/4 × 25 3/4"
Kunstsammlung Nordrhein-Westfalen, Düsseldorf

Léger gave the title *Contrast of Forms* to a number of pictures he painted in 1913 and 1914 that have no representational content whatsoever and deal exclusively with contrasting forms. Though they might be termed "abstract," these forms have a figural character and are treated as objects, as solid, plastic, three-dimensional volumes or, better still, as parts of machines. They are not copied from actual components, but one associates them instinctively with the notion of technology and machinery. It is from these works, if not from the technoid forms of *Nudes in the Forest* (colorplate 1), that a later group of paintings entitled *Mechanical Elements* derived (see colorplate 14). Indeed, their origin may also be sought in the figures of *The Staircase* (colorplate 8), for the fact that the cylindrical forms in that picture represent human shapes is of only secondary importance.

Considering Léger's impassioned interest in reality, it might seem surprising to see him abandon reality completely in these works. But he was convinced that it was just when his art was most unnaturalistic that it most deserved to be termed realistic. In his eyes the criterion of realism was not visible reality but the handling of the artistic medium. He distinguished "visual" realism from "conceptual" realism. The former he considered trivial naturalism, and he never tired of proclaiming: "The realistic value of a work is completely independent of all imitative qualities. This truth must be accepted as a dogma and held up as an axiom for the comprehension of painting in general." What Léger called "conceptual" realism was the notion of the picture as "an arrangement of the three great plastic factors: lines, forms, and colors." He attributed a realistic value to the freedom and autonomy of the pictorial elements because they were in keeping not only with the evolution of art since the days of Manet, the Impressionists, and Cézanne but also with life in the world of today. "Let us gaze wide-eyed at present-day life, which rolls, moves, and overflows alongside us. Let us endeavor to dam it up, canalize it, organize it plastically. A huge task, but feasible. . . . The intensity of the street breaks one's nerves and drives one crazy. . . . Let us organize outer life in our domain: form, color, light." That is Léger's "realistic" justification which enables him to say: "The quality of a painting is directly conditioned by its reality content." But over and above the handling of "form, color, and light," he still felt the urge to make a clear profession of faith in reality by including technoid structures even in "abstract" pictures like this one.

SOLDIER WITH A PIPE

Painted 1916. Oil on canvas, 51 × 38 1/8"
Kunstsammlung Nordrhein-Westfalen, Düsseldorf

When the war broke out in 1914 Léger was mobilized in the sappers. He painted *Soldier with a Pipe* while on leave in Paris in 1916. It is a picture of life in the trenches, of man caught up in the machinery of war. Painted in gray tones on coarse brown canvas, its drab color scheme is relieved only by a touch of warm red in the soldier's face. Here Léger's tubular forms take on a new significance due to the war theme; they seem quite natural when used to represent soldiers engaged in the clash of material resources during World War I. But to realize fully how the human element now prevails over the technical harness in this picture, one must compare it with *The Staircase* (colorplate 8).

Léger himself has told us that the war, with its filth and mud, was for him a period without color, a period of lifelessness, to which he responded with this drab picture. Before the war his art had been full of color, and it became so again once the war was over. But above all else the war was a human experience that exerted a decisive influence over his entire life. By sharing danger and comradeship with his fellow soldiers, Léger came to realize how strongly the common man attracted him. "For me the war of 1914–18 was a stroke of luck," he said over thirty years later. "It enabled me to discover the people and to make an entirely new start. I had the good luck not to be messed up; I was neither happier nor unhappier than the rest and could watch what was going on around me. I was assigned to the Engineers, which, as you know, is a corps of workmen, navvies, miners. Just imagine what a shock that was. I left my studio and the frontiers of art and found myself in the midst of my navvies, with whom I made the whole campaign. It was there that I really and truly understood what a man of the people was. He is a fellow in perfect order: so much so that I realized that I myself was in perfect disorder. . . . I learned their language, for they have a language, a slang. . . . We painters have words and expressions of our own, but our slang is chiefly our pictures. That is why there must be a means for them and us to understand each other. So the point is to renew our ties."

Consequently, the humanization of the technoid forms in *Soldier with a Pipe* is the result of Léger's wartime experience. In his eyes a soldier is neither a heroic fighter nor a hapless victim, but simply a "buddy," involved in the same tragedy as he. But even here, where the experience of reality is what counted most, Léger has not given up his artistic aims for the sake of "expression." At every point the will to form makes itself felt. The human figure is built up of cylindrical shapes, the face is free of any trace of emotion, and the pipe smoke rises in the shape of two spheres. Not one iota of his artistic credo has he renounced. "I discovered the dynamism of mechanics through artillery and tracked vehicles. . . . The breachblock of [that] 75 mm gun opened in the sun taught me more for my artistic evolution than all the museums in the world. Reality in the raw, which burned one. That is where I really grasped the object. So I absorbed that ambience and rendered it as best I could, to suit my pictorial aim. I also thought of my abstractionist studies and got an entirely new idea of the use, function, and destination of abstract art."

THE CARDPLAYERS

Painted 1917. Oil on canvas, 50 3/4 × 76"
Kröller-Müller State Museum, Otterlo

During his convalescence from being gassed Léger painted the large picture entitled *The Cardplayers*. He tells us how it happened:

> It was at war that I got my two feet on the ground. . . . Oh, those big fellows! I was pretty solid myself and I wasn't afraid. I got to be their comrade. Even when I was asked if I wanted to do camouflage work far from the front, I refused to leave them and said: "I'm staying here." When the boys played cards I stayed with them and watched; I did drawings and sketches: I wanted to catch them. Those fellows made a great impression on me and the urge to draw them was quite spontaneous. That was the origin of *The Cardplayers* . . . the first picture for which I deliberately chose a topical subject. I remember working on it in the hospital where I stayed because I had been gassed.

The drawings mentioned in this passage are still extant. Though rather sketchy, they show that Léger was already concerned with the elements of pictorial composition—the rhythmic treatment of the picture plane, the contrasts of light and dark areas, the delineation of smooth planes and solid forms. The drawings keep closer to the "motif," of course. In the painting the genre-like scene, still apparent in the drawings despite the predominance of the will to style, is transmuted into a brilliant interplay of forms. To say that the picture illustrates an anecdote fails to do it justice, for it indicates too great a preoccupation with the concrete material content—soldiers playing cards at a table covered with a yellow cloth; on the left and in the center, two noncommissioned officers in colored uniforms wearing kepis and decorations; on the right, a *poilu* in khaki with a helmet looking on, puffing at his pipe. This is the fraternal male comradeship in which Léger participated so intensely during the war.

The soldier on the right recalls the *Soldier with a Pipe* of 1916 (colorplate 10), but he has undergone a profound change. Human warmth has given way to cold, metallic forms: the figures resemble conglomerates of cylindrical limbs and fragments of limbs, their mighty grippers hardly suitable for holding cards, or robot-like mechanical dummies arrayed in clanking, shiny, steel plates, marked with the stereometric forms of gun barrels. As Léger said,

"Gun barrels, the sun that shines on them, the nakedness of the things themselves—that is what shaped me."

Style has replaced genre. Cézanne's *Cardplayers* of 1890–92 is still a genre picture, even though the accent is on the handling. Léger was a devotee of Cézanne, so he may well have had that picture in mind. Indeed, the contrast between the tall, angular headgear on the left and the flatter, rounded one on the right might be a direct pointer in that direction. But Léger's painting tells us very distinctly that a new century has dawned—an age in which the painter has the same task as the factory worker, namely, to produce plain, clear, precise objects. "A worker," Léger said, "wouldn't dare to deliver a piece that was not precise, smooth, and polished." Thus in his paintings everything is real; even human beings are rendered in terms of naked objects, though they are transformed, fragmented, and denatured by the will of the artist, who has also become an object in this dead object-world. Here—not without a certain irony and a deliberate artistic naiveté—Léger has distinguished the objects by colored details of uniforms, decorations, and insignia of rank, just as he later embellished his acrobats with tattoos that had nothing to do with form.

The Cardplayers is a large, almost monumental painting, the first in that category since *Nudes in the Forest* (colorplate 1). Léger is now on his way to the "grand style" that destined him to be the leading mural painter of the first half of the twentieth century. The "epic" language of the work is heightened by the dynamic, aggressive forms, the dramatic accents, and an abrupt rhythm that is made all the more effective by the inherent tranquillity of the scene—a brief pause in the havoc of war.

One is astonished to see how close this picture is to those painted by the Russian Suprematist Kasimir Malevich in 1912—*Woman with Pails*, with its cylindrical forms, and, more particularly, *Scissors Grinder*, with the head faceted in a Futurist manner and hands designed like machine components. Actually, in *The Cardplayers* Léger was closer to Malevich than to any other painter. The latter's pictures had been executed five years earlier, but no evidence has yet been found that Léger was acquainted with them, even from reproductions.

COLORPLATE 12

THE ACROBATS

Painted 1918. Oil on canvas, 38 1/8 × 46 1/8''
Kunstmuseum, Basel

This picture was painted in 1918. There is an earlier version from that same year and a later one from 1920. The year that elapsed between *The Cardplayers* (colorplate 11) and this version had brought a further condensation in Léger's stylistic mediums, but it also initiated a new trend from three-dimensionality to flatness. Here Léger has tackled the human figure with a directness that makes even *The Cardplayers* smack of tradition. The distance that separates us from the figures is eliminated and we are now quite close to them. And yet we remain outside the stagelike picture space which, despite the presence of the spectators—shown "on a higher level" rather than "in the distance"—does not open toward the rear. In *The Cardplayers* the figures still enclosed a concave oval space; here they plunge toward us out of their frame. They form an irreconcilable contrast with the richly articulated background, whose surface has now been given an ornamental character made up of colored geometric areas, dotted, striped, and plain. Flatness mingles with perspective, but the cubic and cylindrical elements that alternately advance and recede do not break up the plane so much as they irritate and activate it. Representational and purely ornamental details are juxtaposed, and two big typographic characters borrowed from posterwork appear like symbols of modern urban civilization. The clear, emphatic language reflects Léger's abhorrence of ambiguity, which also caused him to lay such stress on the foreground.

The approach to the colors, too, is rather more direct than in *The Cardplayers*. They are more varied, brighter, more metallic. The object quality, the modeling of the volumes—all the features that gave *The Cardplayers* its unique character—are more in evidence here. Moreover, the composition is tauter: a vertical pipe cuts off one quarter of the picture plane and provides a firm stay. The forms are more geometrical, but this new trend toward geometrization counteracts, as regards both form and color, the intense agitation of the various elements.

This varied interplay of colored forms has virtually deprived the acrobatic act of all significance. The human being has become a lay figure immersed in a complicated mosaic of simple forms. Not a trace is left of the romantic atmosphere of the circus tent that has fascinated so many artists since the end of the nineteenth century. But one cannot help recalling one of the most famous circus pictures of modern times—Georges Seurat's *Circus* of 1891. Actually, Léger may well have had it in mind when he painted his own acrobats. There, too, a central human figure—a clown with head turned sideways—is cut off by the lower edge of the picture; there, too, the figure stands almost outside the picture space and seems to be "stage managing" the scene; there, too, spectators are seated in the distance; and even the motif of the stairway by their side is common to both works. If one is tempted to believe that in *The Cardplayers* Léger's intention was to bring Cézanne's rendering of that subject up to date, one cannot avoid the feeling that here he has done the same for Seurat's big circus picture.

(BOTTOM)

THE DISKS

Painted 1918. Oil on canvas, 94 1/2 × 71"
Musée d'Art Moderne de la Ville de Paris

Does *The Disks*, one of the major works Léger produced immediately after the war and during the early stage of his "Mechanical Period," represent a machine? Unquestionably the many disks, large and small, are more than mere circular forms; they are combined with rods, levers, and pipes to make up a dynamic mechanism. But it is a mechanism freely invented by the artist. "In my search for brilliance and intensity," he said, "I have made use of the machine just as others happen to employ the nude figure or the still life."

One must never be dominated by the subject. . . . I have never amused myself by copying a machine. I invent pictures of machines as others conjure up landscapes in their imagination. For me the mechanical element is not a predilection or an attitude but a means to impart a feeling of force and power. . . . One must retain the utilizable part of the subject and turn that part to good account. I try to make a *handsome object* out of the mechanical elements.

Léger was a pictorial engineer, not a mechanical engineer. But he found inspiration in the precision, polish, dynamism, and functionality of the machine.

"Walk around the Machine Show—for, like artists, machines, too, have their annual show—go and see the Automobile Show, the Aircraft Show, the Paris Trade Fair; they are the finest shows on earth." Léger's impassioned acceptance of the machine was in direct opposition to the attitude of Francis Picabia and other Dadaist painters, who poked fun at the machine about that time. For them the machine symbolized a rationality that they rejected as an intellectual principle; for Léger, it was not inconsistent with his artistic rationalism.

To Léger the machine was first and foremost the application of geometrical law. "Modern man," he wrote in 1924, "lives more and more in a preponderant geometrical order. All man's mechanical and industrial creation depends on geometrical needs." What he painted in *The Disks* was not so much a machine as the "preponderant geometrical order" of the machine world. Here the major motif is the circle. One can see a trend toward circular forms from the very first signs of geometrization and elementarization in

Léger's art. The trend was already apparent in pictures like *The Smokers* of 1911 (colorplate 3) and *Woman in Blue* of 1912 (colorplate 4). And in this picture circles are the predominant feature; they have become more geometrical, are more numerous, and are framed by broad colored bands. Even when broken or fragmentary, they are still recognizable as colored segments.

During the first postwar years, while fascinated by the rediscovery of color, Léger kept up a dialogue with his friend Delaunay. Before the war Delaunay had made a start on his *formes circulaires*. In his eyes the circle was *the* absolute form, the colored circle *the* symbol of light. Léger, though undoubtedly influenced by Delaunay's suns and moons, was quite free of his sort of light symbolism; he loved colors for their own sake without endowing them with a symbolic content. But he did feel the light in colors: not Delaunay's pure light, but the light of the modern world. "The epoch of the nude, of light. No more taste for the dubious, mystic-oriental lure of chiaroscuro. The indiscrete projector lamp. The floodlights of the film studio. The Sun." Not Delaunay's cosmic, "Orphic" suns but colored machine wheels that revolve around their axes, driven by motors, in clear, pure, opaque colors, more like railroad and street signals than solar prisms. "We are faced at present with an unprecedented invasion by useful, multicolored objects. Even the farm machine has become a pleasant person and dresses up like a butterfly or a bird. Color is such a vital necessity that it is reasserting its rights everywhere."

In this picture the forms have become flat; they are no longer spheres but disks, no longer pipes but tapes. Yet corporeal elements perspectively rendered crop up here and there; the dynamism of the machine picture does not let the forms come to geometrical rest on the picture plane. A dynamic effect is also achieved by the many overlapping and fragmented forms and the crisscrossing of diagonals and circles. And here too, as in *The Acrobats* (colorplate 12), the major motif occupies the foreground. Quite obviously the scene is set in a machine shed; the machine stands in front, and in the background—contrasting with the machine's diagonal composition—is a horizontally and vertically articulated wall barred by cast-iron railings.

MECHANICAL ELEMENTS

Painted 1918–23. Oil on canvas, 83 1/8 × 66"
Kunstmuseum, Basel

If in *The Disks* (colorplate 13) Léger proclaimed his acceptance of the law of flatness, he violated it in this picture with its violent gestures of sharply modeled plastic forms. Here, too, he has set a complex conglomerate of gleaming machine components in front of a geometrically articulated backdrop: the painter has turned into a machine fitter. However, the assembled parts do not add up to a "real" engine but to a purely pictorial, almost ornamental structure. What is true of this major work of Léger's "Mechanical Period" is equally true of the other pictures he painted at that time and entitled *Motors*.

In this picture, as in *The Disks*, man is banned from the machine world, for, to use Léger's own words, "the event of today is the personality of objects. They come more and more to the fore, while man disappears behind them." Man was soon to find his voice again in Léger's art and ultimately to become its dominant factor. Here he has done his job and the work remains to prove it: man can be present without being seen.

Léger felt that in the art of his generation the subject was being dislodged and replaced by the object. Of course, a traditional still life also relied on objects, but they were parts of a pervasive context, elements of a "subject" called "still life." Léger's artistic vision snatched the object from its environment, freed it from its bonds, and isolated and personalized it.

One can view the evolution of art today as a fifty-year struggle between the notion of the subject, as understood by the Italian Renaissance, and the interest for the object and for pure color that is becoming more and more substantiated in our modern ideas. . . . This object, which was imprisoned in the subject, is breaking free. . . . It is becoming the chief character in the new painting. . . . Ancient painting is the subject and, as I see it, contemporary art is the object. . . . To extricate the object from the subject, isolate it, give it a plastic value by comparing it with contrasting forms, that is the new, very contemporary picture one must make.

It was not long before this cult of the object in Léger's oeuvre took forms that were different from those in this picture, where the subject—a machine in a shed—is not yet completely eliminated. Still, the metal elements are more radically isolated here than the limbs of his human figures in pictures of the previous years. The composition predicates the decomposition of the object. The structure, functional if not capable of functioning, is put together piece by piece. This assembly work obeys pictorial laws and not the law of reality, though that is the law which governs the spirit of the picture.

THE CITY

Painted 1919–20. Oil on canvas, 90 3/4 × 117 1/4"
Philadelphia Museum of Art. The A. E. Gallatin Collection

Before the war Léger painted villages in a vein that was neither romantic nor idyllic; they merely provided scope for his colored "spheres, cones, and cylinders." After the wartime experience, in the euphoria that accompanied his new awareness of modern reality, his art demanded new materials and a new intensity that could only be found in a big city. For Léger the city signified modernity, dynamism, geometry, and color. "After the war," he said, "walls, streets, objects suddenly became intensely colored. The houses dressed up in blue, yellow, red. Gigantic letters were written on them. That is radiant, brutal modern life." He went on to tell of the "polychrome invasion" that took place at that time: "Color rushes in like a torrent. It swallows up the walls, the streets. . . . When one opens a window, a piece of shrill publicity blows in with the wind. . . . Exuberance of color and noise." Léger was profoundly concerned with the notion of colored houses and walls and welcomed the researches that modern architects made along those lines about 1925.

It was in this spirit that in 1919–20 he painted the big picture entitled *The City*—a strongly geometrized composition of flat tracts of brilliant color and greatly emphasized verticals indicating houses, steel structures, a port, posters, traffic lights, and huge stencil letters. Léger's consummate mastery of his medium enabled him to make order out of the chaos of the modern city, with signals of reality flashing up here and there. His aim was not to render the fantastic vision of a metropolis but "to discover a more orderly pictorial arrangement, the contrary of the confusion of advertisements that slash the streets of modern towns. The ideal is to achieve a feeling of beauty, balance, physical and spiritual liberation." And in the context of this picture: "*The City* is painted in flat, pure colors. Letters are introduced as realistic values. In this picture I have avoided using the complementary colors that Robert Delaunay has insisted on retaining. . . . To preserve the color's tonal and constructive force I had to avoid the complementary relationships of Impressionism."

At that time Picasso himself went in for a Cubism of colored patches that culminated in the *Three Musicians* of 1921. But he did not succumb to the lure of technology and the metropolis initiated by the Italian Futurists. In 1911 Umberto Boccioni had painted his *Forces of a Street*, in which he extolled the dynamism of the great city in terms that were both expressive and pathetic but reserved where color was concerned. There is no artistic link between Léger and Boccioni; but Léger was even further away from the elegiac wavering between yesterday and today, between antiquity and the steel age, that was typical of the dreamlike visions painted by Giorgio de Chirico before 1920. Once again he is very close to Robert Delaunay. Delaunay had painted his monumental *City of Paris*—three huge Graces in a dense mosaic of colored planes and cubes—in 1910–12; he had already produced his Eiffel Tower series; and, more important still, he had inserted huge poster letters in his big *Cardiff Team* of 1912–13. But Léger's calm composition contrasts with Delaunay's lyricism; his clear, "cool" colors, with Delaunay's nuanced palette; his renunciation of action in favor of "pure" forms, with Delaunay's scenic action. The two male figures that climb the stairs so mechanically in Léger's *The City* are only a secondary motif compared with the violent action of Delaunay's ballplayers. Léger was interested, not in human action, but in the action of colored forms.

In his picture of 1920–21 entitled *The Disks in the City*, Léger combined elements from *The Disks* of 1918 (colorplate 13) with others from *The City* of 1919–20. By employing certain elements of one work in others, a procedure he adopted very frequently right up to the end of his life, Léger stressed their nature as isolated, independent objects which, like movable stage properties, could be utilized in various productions.

Léger himself wrote about this picture:

After the war, in 1919, in *The City* I composed a picture exclusively with pure, flat colors. Technically, that picture was a plastic revolution. One could achieve depth and dynamism without modulation or chiaroscuro. It was advertising that first drew the consequences. The pure tones of the blues, reds, and yellows break away from this picture and invade posters, shop windows, roadside signs, and traffic lights. Color had become free. It was a reality in its own right. It had a new activity, entirely independent of the objects which, till then, had contained and supported it.

With this picture and others of the same period, Léger undoubtedly exerted a great influence on advertising and shop-window layout.

THE MECHANIC

Painted 1920. Oil on canvas, 45 1/2 × 35"
The National Gallery of Canada, Ottawa

Only four years elapsed between Léger's *Soldier with a Pipe* of 1916 (colorplate 10) and The *Mechanic* of 1920. In both pictures men of the people are depicted smoking a pipe or cigarette, but they are viewed from totally different angles. The mechanic is no longer enclosed in a protective space; like the machines in *The Disks* (colorplate 13) and *Mechanical Elements* (colorplate 14), he stands before a geometrically articulated wall without space or atmosphere. Moreover, he is no longer enveloped in painting; the colors are plain and unadorned, as if in a vacuum, deprived entirely of the rich nuances of the wartime picture. The mechanic seems more solid than the soldier, despite the latter's cylindrical forms; his hands seem huger, thanks to their more anatomical conformation, and unwieldier than the soldier's steel fists. But what strikes one most in *The Mechanic* is the vivid contrast between the colored geometry of the background and the colorless plasticity of the human figure. In *Soldier with a Pipe* the angled posture gives the figure a certain accidental, momentary quality; here it is rigorously frontal with the head in profile, so that the scope of the flat portrayal is exploited as in an Egyptian relief. The posture has a certain absolute finality that extends beyond the momentary workbreak. Unlike the soldier in a peaceful moment, what we have here is, not a man like so many others, but a mechanic, pure and simple.

The "naive" quality of the picture, due to the majestic mustache, the bulging muscles, and the tattooed left arm, deserves a word of comment. One is put in mind of Henri Rousseau le Douanier, in whose pictures, including his self-portrait, there are so many mustaches. It is as if one of Rousseau's figures had served Léger as model; or, perhaps, one of the rigorously frontal mustachioed men in pictures like *Country Wedding* of 1905 or *Ballplayers* of 1908 had turned, no less rigorously, to side view. Léger met Rousseau through Delaunay about the time he was painting *Nudes in the Forest*, and he called on him frequently. It is hardly credible that he did not think of Rousseau when he was drawing the deliberately naive figure of his mechanic.

But another character who comes to mind when we look at *The Mechanic* is Charlie Chaplin, with his candor, his masklike face, his anonymity, his mechanical movements. The poet Guillaume Apollinaire took Léger to see his first Chaplin film and Léger was enormously impressed. "It was Apollinaire," he wrote later, "who took me to see Charlie Chaplin when I was on leave from the front. . . . I was flabbergasted: that funny little guy who succeeds in being not only a funny little guy but a sort of living puppet, dry, jerky, black-and-white. Nothing of the theater actor. . . . He was the first image-man. . . . He belongs to the great tradition of the ancients and of primitive peoples who invented the mask. He has ousted the individual from the screen." In another context Léger said: "Charlie Chaplin is universal because he is visual. The starting point is Charlie as a mechanism." That Chaplin fascinated Léger is also proved by the illustrations he did for Ivan Goll's *Chapliniade* (1920) and the Charlie Chaplin passage in his own film *Ballet mécanique* of 1924.

COLORPLATE 17

MAN WITH A PIPE

Painted 1920. Oil on canvas, 51 1/8 × 77 5/8''
Galerie Beyeler, Basel

Unlike the Cubists, Léger never did collages. In this picture, however, he "stuck together" two half-pictures that seemingly belong in different contexts. One shows a man standing on a platform smoking a pipe; the chief feature of the other is a wide staircase. And within these two major parts the various flat elements seem to be cut out and pasted on, an effect found also in *The City* (colorplate 15), which was painted not long before. Léger was concerned at that time with the fragmentation not only of objects but also of geometric planes. Other planes intrude themselves, and we seldom find a circle so clear and intact as the yellow-red signal in the right-hand section of the picture. These multiple intersections do not suggest space, but they provide a sense of movement to an art rendered motionless by the mediums it employs.

The composition as a whole displays few directions—vertical, horizontal, diagonal. But these directions are strongly stressed and give a stable, amply articulated framework to the picture. The diagonals give an impression of three-dimensional space in the platform and the staircase. But these features, too, are treated in the flat and do not furnish indications of a central-perspective layout of the entire picture space. No spatial unity can be seen in the whole picture, nor even in its two halves taken separately: one's eye is always brought back to the plane. And, by the same token, the predominance of the pictorial language makes it more difficult to identify the setting. The big life buoy might indicate that we are on a ship, but the male figure gives us no further information.

Here once again we have a man smoking during a work-break, like the soldier in the picture of 1916, the cardplayers of 1917, and the mechanic of 1920. In strong contrast to his brightly colored surroundings, he is painted gray on gray, with no differentiation between body and clothes. Unlike all the other forms, which are treated in the flat, he is solidly modeled. He is put together, after the manner of the soldiers in *The Cardplayers* (colorplate 11), in separate stereometric pieces with no organic unity. Indeed, to make sure that one doesn't get the feeling that something might possibly exist outside the picture too, the various parts are clearly dissected at the joints. It is the picture that imposes its law on man, forcing him to move "unnaturally" and to hold his pipe in a quite impossible fashion. The smoke rises in three spheres that once again call to mind *Soldier with a Pipe* of 1916 (colorplate 10) and *The City* of 1919–20 (colorplate 15).

The man has been completely divested of his individuality: he is an anonymous worker in a workaday world. The head is a sphere with hair, nose, eyes, and mouth, but no emotions. The soldiers and the acrobats in Léger's earlier paintings are also expressionless, but since the fragmentation of the forms disrupts the faces, there can be no question of human expression. Here, instead, Léger has risked giving the man a human aspect; he has left him his face and gaze, so that one cannot help seeing the lack of expression as an empty expression and therefore as an expression of a certain type. One has only to cover the head for a moment to become aware of an expression that was perhaps not intended by the artist but is very effective nonetheless—an expression that lies in a totally different dimension from all the other elements of the picture.

There is a second, very similar version of *Man with a Pipe*, with a dog feeding between the life buoy and the circle.

MAN WITH A DOG

Painted 1921. Oil on canvas, 25 1/2 × 36"
Collection Mr. and Mrs. Nathan Cummings, New York City

Between 1920 and 1922 Léger painted a number of upright and oblong pictures that he called *paysages animés* —landscapes animated by a few humans and animals—in which the traditional, realistic motif of the human figure in a landscape finds a new formulation (see figs. 21–23). Léger treated scenery in the manner best suited to his artistic aims; he sought nature precisely where it is inhabited and transformed by man. His big forest of 1909–10 (colorplate 1) is already "animated" by the woodcutters and transformed by the axes they wield. In *Railroad Crossing* of 1912–13 (colorplate 5) he has "civilized" nature by means of the crossing gates. The village pictures of 1913 and 1914 (colorplates 6, 7) are prevented from becoming nature idylls by the houses—not to mention the painter's own intervention in the matter of form. After his "Mechanical Period," Léger was once again attracted to the landscape, but civilization had left its mark and it was denatured by "ugly" house fronts, steel structures, and poster lettering.

Here Léger gives us a picture of the modern industrial landscape, in which men move about as anonymously and robot-like as the astronauts on the surface of the moon almost half a century later. The two men are once again painted gray on gray before the motley background of house and country. They are merely featureless mechanical cogs in the productive machine, whether industrial or agricultural. In fact, agriculture and industry are depicted side by side—the cows beside the iron gate, the winding tower (if that is what it is) beside the trees. A plastic pall of

industrial smoke rises above the scene and the letters of the advertisement flash up on the wall of the house—"the hard, dry poster panel, violent colors, stencil letters, that cut a harmonious landscape," as Léger said. "These villages, colored by posters, these landscapes where factories smoke, where trains and airplanes pass by, where cranes turn and machines work . . . the transformation of nature by man." Or again: "I maintain that the poster, as a modern element which cuts through a mellow, sentimental landscape, is a splendid modern motif in art. It is a contrast. The hard value heightens the soft value."

For all this transformation and civilization of nature, a picture like *Man with a Dog* has a certain ideal quality paralleled by the hieratically ideal figures in *Three Women (Le Grand Déjeuner)*, painted in the same year (colorplate 19). The dominance of color and form not only subdues the genre quality of the scene; it elevates it to a "higher" plane, the plane of the popular amateur theater with its naive, idealizing sets. Civilization goes hand in hand with rusticity, the modern workaday world with the impression of Arcadian peace in which one already senses Léger's later social utopianism.

The increasing importance of the human being in Léger's oeuvre—particularly in such a stagelike setting as here— must be considered in the context of his collaboration with Rolf de Maré's Swedish Ballet. In 1922 he designed the sets and costumes for *Skating Rink* (music by Arthur Honegger); and in 1923 for *La Création du monde* (music by Darius Milhaud).

THREE WOMEN (LE GRAND DÉJEUNER)

Painted 1921. Oil on canvas, 72 1/4 × 99"
The Museum of Modern Art, New York City
Mrs. Simon Guggenheim Fund

After the mechanical period came the monumental period, the massive phase, the compositions with large figures, the enlargement of the details. I heightened the impression of flatness while arranging my figures and objects in the same formal manner as during the machine period, minus the dynamism. I had broken down the human body, so I set about putting it together again and rediscovering the human face. . . . I wanted a rest, a breathing space. After the dynamism of the mechanical period, I felt a need for the staticity of large figures.

As early as 1920 Léger produced a number of pictures with static female figures—not only groups composed of one recumbent and one erect figure, but single figures too (see figs. 24, 25). In them the human forms, however object-like they still remain and however much they are governed by the law of the picture, form the principal motif. Like *Man with a Pipe* (colorplate 17) and *Man with a Dog* (colorplate 18), the figures are mostly painted in grisaille. Among these works are two very similar ones entitled *Odalisques*, in which two female nudes viewed from the front, one standing, the other reclining, form a cross in the middle of the picture plane. In another painting, entitled *The Teacup*, a seated woman faces the spectator, a cup in her hand and a book on her lap. Léger combined these two arrangements in *Three Women (Le Grand Déjeuner)* of 1921.

The two recumbent nudes are painted gray, the seated nude is brown. The plain colors and rounded modeling contrast with the motley geometry of the setting. The floor pattern, though treated in the flat—in parallel perspective—gives an impression of depth without infringing the strict law of flatness. The statuesque quality of the figures enhances the static quality of the composition, from which all trace of movement is banned. Each member, each object, is treated as a pure form. For instance, in the reclining woman in front, the head is treated as a sphere, the hair as a wave, the neck as a cone, the breasts as two spheres, the forearm as the segment of a circle. If the anatomy (but not the form) grows confused on the right, that is quite in order because the anatomy of the picture is basically different from the anatomy of the human figure.

Here too, and more emphatically than in *Man with a Pipe*, the lack of expression in the faces that gaze into the void is most expressive, though not in the sense that the painter has tried to produce an individual "expression." It stems from his reduction of the human face to its most elemental form and his refusal to denature that face by interfering with its form. The silent gravity of the faces combines with the monumental frontality of the figures to produce a grand, hieratic effect, compared with which the scene—three women at breakfast—is quite unimportant. True, Léger said that "for me the human figure, the human body, counts no more than keys or bicycles. That's true.

For me they are plastically valid objects to arrange as I like." But obviously he here gives the figures a preponderant role in the composition and statement of the picture. No longer faceted or fragmented, they face the spectator modeled in the round.

The objects too are simplified, depicted with the utmost precision, entire and intact, purged of all climatic, atmospheric, and calligraphic factors, and devoid of formal manipulation as well. This purification of forms and objects brings Léger very close to the Purists Amédée Ozenfant and Charles-Édouard Jeanneret (Le Corbusier), with whom he was on friendly terms at the time and who had already published their Purist manifesto *After Cubism* in 1918.

Thus, here again Léger has applied in a broader fashion the law of "multiplicative contrasts" in which he so firmly believed. "To achieve the maximum intensity and even violence on a wall is my ultimate goal. . . . I can only obtain that intensity by ruthlessly employing the most absolute contrasts—flat elements in pure colors, modeled elements in grisaille, realistic objects."

In works like *Three Women* Léger began to develop a new grand figure style, which put him in line with the classic tradition of French painting. That was also the time of Picasso's "Classical Period." In his works, too, huge female figures make their appearance; but Picasso, unlike Léger, portrays them in classical drapery, at a mythological distance, and in a naturalistic manner. The taste for the colossal that is so apparent in *Three Women*, particularly in the seated figure with shapeless thighs, and which was already foreshadowed in such early works as *Nudes in the Forest* (colorplate 1) can also be observed in Picasso. But to Picasso's classicist, mythologizing bent Léger opposed —despite the icon-like solemnity of his figures—a resolute, clearly stated modernity that was not lessened even by the kinship of the motif with Édouard Manet's *Olympia* of 1863, with the recumbent naked woman, the standing Negro servant, and the black cat, which any French painter could paint with his eyes shut. Incidentally, there is a replica of the cat in Léger's language at the foot of the bed in *Three Women*.

Seven years later, in 1928, he delivered a lecture in Berlin in which he said:

When this civilization has reached its plenitude and its equilibrium, we shall witness, I hope, the advent of a new religion: the cult of the Beauty in which we live and which we create. A concrete, objective idealism that will replace advantageously the old religions whose aim has always been to put the world to sleep with the opium of a fallacious future life that remains to be proved. Hereafter we shall live in light, clarity, nakedness. Then we shall find a totally new font of joy, which is our future.

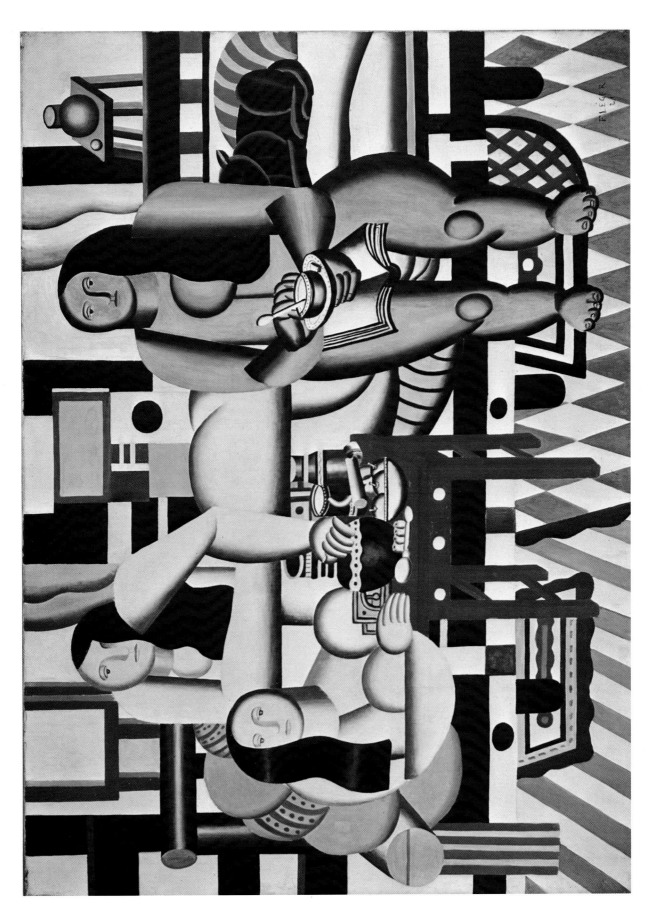

(BOTTOM)

MOTHER AND CHILD

Painted 1922. Oil on canvas, 67 3/8 × 95''
Kunstmuseum, Basel

This picture, no less masterly than *Three Women* (colorplate 19), was painted exactly ten years after *Woman in Blue* (colorplate 4), but the two have virtually nothing in common. During the interval Léger underwent a complete change without losing his identity; rather, in order to find it. In the earlier painting the female figure is concealed by geometric planes and fragmented to such an extent as to be all but unrecognizable; now it faces the spectator almost lifesize. The blue planes have been transmuted into massive blue volumes. The only abstract elements still allowed refer to concrete objects—a paneled door, a chest of drawers, a banister. But before the figure could be recomposed as we see it here, it had to undergo a total decomposition. And in both works the decomposition is equally visible in the figure and in the picture as a whole.

The woman reclines on a lozenge-patterned deck chair opened out flat in obedience to the law of the picture. The drapery is arranged in large, simple volumes. The huge, balloon-shaped arms hang like heavy weights ending in four-fingered hands. Both the woman and the child have rigid, masklike faces, as in *Three Women*, but here they are still more precisely drawn, more naked, stiffer, and colder.

Inanimate objects are given more importance; they are distributed in three still-life groups in the center and at both sides of the picture. The scrupulous accuracy with which the familiar objects are painted denotes a more than normally developed perception, and their isolation in a vacuum heightens their visual significance. They are stylized to the point of formulas and schemas and reduced to mere ornamental values. "When I transfer an object from the drawing to the painting," Léger once said, "I simplify it. I subject its form to the general idea of the picture, divest it of all superfluity, free it from all parasites that might interfere with the purity of the reception." This makes it interesting to compare the painting with the pencil drawing, which is fortunately still extant.

Léger treated in exactly the same way exteriors and interiors, nature and the world of objects; his picture space is a vacuum in which there is no atmosphere to confuse forms and colors. Nature, too, is viewed "objectively"—not in the descriptive sense of the word but as a sum of objects, such as hills and trees. It is just as stiff and lifeless as the human faces. Léger was interested not in the liveliness of nature but in the liveliness of the picture, and that depends on the highly contrasted interplay of all the elements present, both abstract and figurative. Even the more lively shaped cactus on the left is stiffened to the point of lifelessness. Its turgid, rigid forms, like those of the trees in some Animated Landscapes of 1921, put one in mind—and not by chance—of the tropical plants painted by Henri Rousseau.

COLORPLATE 21

THE BIG BARGE

Painted 1923. Oil on canvas, 49 1/4 × 74 3/4"
Musée National Fernand Léger, Biot

It is typical of Léger that, besides elaborating his pictures in pencil studies, he often executed several paintings before reaching the definitive version. Many of his works exist in a number of variants. Very often, too, he inserted elements of one picture almost unchanged in another or utilized the basic formula of one as part of another, more complex work. His art is not a spontaneous, brilliant flash of creation, nor an adventure lightheartedly embarked on that provided him with a steady stream of surprises. It is essentially purposeful, adjusted to the "object" (the definitive work) rather than to the subject (the artist himself). It is because he objectified his pictorial inventions as pictorial formulas that Léger was free to dispose of them as objects to suit his artistic purpose.

The Big Barge is the last of a long line of pictures executed between 1920 and 1923 whose theme could not fail to fascinate Léger. The world of the watermen who navigate the French canals and rivers has a popular poetry all its own that embraces nature, technology, and human beings. Léger has centered his picture on the barge, which

he has depicted as he did the motors in his machine pictures. The hills, houses, factories, and trees serve merely to set off the craft in the foreground, which is built up of overlapping planes of different shapes and colors, forming a pictorially decorative rather than a technically functional structure. Instead of "floating" on the surface of the water, it "stands" on the surface of the picture. The various forms, the bright colors, and the many ornamental textures counteract the static composition of poster-like planes. All the elements of the picture are treated in the flat except for the schematically modeled, undulating gray hills and the spherical green trees.

Compared with earlier barge pictures, quite apart from the absence of man and beast and the diminished importance of the landscape, there is evident a growing tendency to flatness, clarity, simplicity, and grand vision. The idiom is that of the fresco painter, and this development in Léger's work squares with his growing concern for wall painting and design.

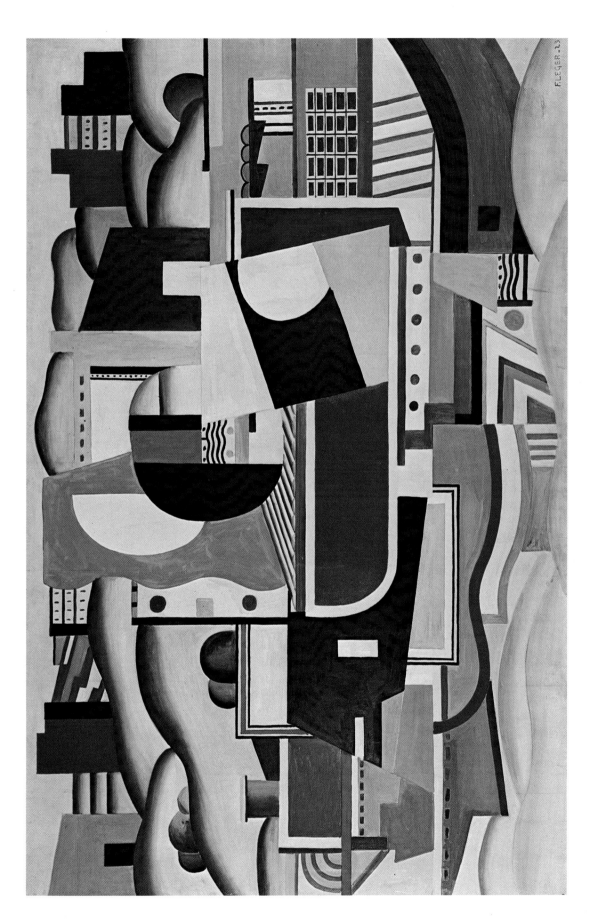

(BOTTOM)

THE READERS

Painted 1924. Oil on canvas, 45 × 57 1/2''
Musée National d'Art Moderne, Paris

Léger used to tell the following story:

When I brought Rosenberg *The Readers*, I was very short of cash. He looked at the picture and all he said was: "But the woman has no hair! Do be reasonable and give her a little. She looks as if she has been scalped and it's not a pleasant sight." And he insisted. But, do as I would, I simply couldn't give the woman any hair. In the place occupied by her head I needed a plain round form. I wasn't being willful, but I couldn't add a hair.

This story shows very clearly what Léger considered artistically necessary: what was pleasant or agreeable meant nothing to him. Owing to this stern rejection of what was agreeable, Léger's pictures displeased a great many people; they still do. He took that risk in his stride with the self-confidence of a man who knows that it is a question not only of truth but of beauty as well. "The cult of the beautiful is of course a possibility. On that point I agree with the theories we are indebted to Ozenfant for; the longing for the beautiful is with us everywhere and every day; it simply cannot be denied." But the beauty of a girl is not the beauty of a picture.

In *The Readers* Léger took another step forward. The heads are treated still more schematically than before. The still-life setting in the large figure pieces of 1921 and 1922 has been replaced by a few planes delimited by geometrical figures. The bright colors have yielded to a more reserved, severe palette. The image is much more ascetic. The objects are treated like symbols; the totally denatured flowers are held like a scepter. All this matches the women's solemn, serious mien.

Léger has viewed the figures from closer up, but that only makes them more alien: the nearness emphasizes their masklike appearance, which at a greater distance would be influenced by perspective. The space between the spectator and the figures in *Three Women* (colorplate 19) and *Mother and Child* (colorplate 20), which leaves the figures secure in their proper surroundings, is here greatly reduced. The effect is like that of a shot taken by a camera right on the subject.

As a matter of fact, Léger was greatly interested in the cinema just then, particularly in the close-up. He had first encountered it through Abel Gance's *La Roue* of 1921, which he saw being shot. In 1923 he had collaborated on the sets for Marcel L'Herbier's *L'Inhumaine* and in 1924 made a film of his own entitled *Ballet mécanique*. What interested Léger in the close-up was that it extracts an object from the subject, even a detail from the object, and makes it stand alone; he couldn't help being fascinated by this. Thereafter, when he magnified and isolated a detail in a painting it was not only for reasons of style but also because of his encounter with the cinema.

Thus he suddenly began to pay attention to a detail of the human body that had been rarely considered in the history of art and seldom even in his own oeuvre—the fingernail. Most details he overlooked as of secondary importance and therefore superfluous, but from now on he never ceased to lay the utmost emphasis on this one. How far his fascination went is proved by the following passage:

I photograph the fingernail of a modern woman very precisely under a very strong light. This extremely well-tended nail is treated with no less care than her eye or her mouth. It is an object that has an intrinsic value. Now I project this nail onto the screen magnified a hundred times and say to one person: "Look, this is a fragment of a nascent planet." To another: "This is an abstract form." They will both be very surprised and enthusiastic. They will take my word for it. In the end I shall tell them: "No, what you have just seen is the nail of the little finger of my wife's left hand." They will be annoyed but will never again ask the famous question: "What does that represent?"

(BOTTOM)

THREE FIGURES

Painted 1924. Oil on canvas, 51 × 51''
Private collection, Switzerland

Still more ascetic than the preceding picture is this group of three figures, two women and a man, also painted in 1924. Here Léger has renounced color altogether. The figures of both sexes are brown; the background is an undifferentiated gray plane without either representational or nonrepresentational pattern. The symbolic aspect of the figures is still further emphasized. The woman on the left holds a rod; its significance is not clear, but over and above its obvious function as a pictorial value, it gives the impression of being a ceremonial staff. The man holds a scroll after the manner of an orator in ancient Rome. Though here the significance of these emblems is not clear, they were once emblems of significance.

The figures—one standing, one kneeling, one seated— are squat. The limbs are placed one next to the other like independent volumes. The cylinder, still predominant in *Three Women* (colorplate 19), has been replaced by balloon-like forms that seem somehow more "organic." Here too the fingers give the impression of being screwed on, and together with the nails they form a lively contrast with the broad, flat bodies. One has only to concentrate on the four hands with their fingers and nails and on the stable base provided by the three feet to realize the forceful rhythm they give to the static picture. Force is what counts in this picture, and for it even such athletic nudes as these require no muscles. This does not contradict the muscular appearance of *The Mechanic* of 1920 (colorplate 16). whose muscles—owing precisely to their exaggeration and stylization—are at once more and less than muscles.

The group resembles a tautly designed bas-relief on a flat ground and therefore calls to mind the art of ancient Egypt or Assyria. Léger never tired of insisting that modern artists must pass over the "decadence" of the Renaissance and hark back to those decisive cultures. "Our traditions— if traditions are really necessary—are the ancient cultures, the primitives, the Egyptians, the early Greeks, the folk arts." And again: "All the ancient cultures—Chaldean, Egyptian, Chinese, Romanesque, Gothic—were ages of invention. . . . Those primitives knew how to use the human elements round about them in all freedom, without being dominated by them."

Henri Rousseau was a primitive too. Léger knew him well and loved his work. The man on the left in *Three Figures* was undoubtedly inspired by the portrait of Apollinaire in Rousseau's *The Poet and His Muse* of 1909 in that the poet has a similar expression and a similar pose and carries a scroll in his left hand.

How persistently Léger continued to work on a schema once he had discovered it is shown by the fact that in a painting of 1927 there is an almost identical group of figures set against a bright red ground; the later figures, however, are more frontal, erect, and monumental.

COLORPLATE 24

THE SIPHON

Painted 1924. Oil on canvas, 36 1/4 × 23 5/8"
Collection Mrs. Arthur C. Rosenberg, Chicago

Léger turned away from the subject to the object during his Cubist phase and more radically still during his "Mechanical Period." Paradoxically enough, he seems to have been most enthralled by the object at the very moment he again allowed the subject a little play. Examples of this are the scrupulously depicted still lifes in *Three Women* of 1921 (colorplate 19) and *Mother and Child* of 1922 (colorplate 20). In *The Readers* of 1924 (colorplate 22) the figures are attacked at close quarters; this is also true of objects at that time. Bottles and glasses, fruit dishes and pipes, hats and umbrellas, flowers and keys, all are taken from their context and become the major characters in the picture. To use his own words, Léger isolated and personalized his objects, and before painting them he did extremely detailed drawings. At the art school he set up in 1924 with Amédée Ozenfant, the spokesman of the Purist movement, he admonished his pupils to draw objects with the greatest possible precision.

"In 1923 and 1924," he wrote, "I executed pictures using as active elements objects isolated from all trace of atmosphere or of mutual relationships—objects taken from abandoned subjects. The subject had already been destroyed in painting, just as the avant-garde cinema had destroyed the script. . . . I thought that the neglected, unconsidered object was capable of replacing the subject."

It was chiefly the close-up, which he welcomed with such enthusiasm, that helped Léger to discover the object and its fragments as values in their own right. "The cinema personalizes and frames the fragment; this new realism could have incalculable consequences. A collar stud under the projector magnified a hundred times becomes a radiant planet. A totally new lyricism of the transformed object is born. . . . . The future of both the cinema and painting depends on the interest it will confer on objects, fragments of objects, and purely fantastic and imaginary inventions." Léger had denounced the subject as the error of painting; now he denounced the script as the error of the cinema.

The object's newly won significance could not be rendered more cogently than by the cut-off human hand that squirts soda water into a glass. This is tantamount to using the close-up as a means of self-expression. What we have here is not a still life in the traditional sense, with objects arranged on a table. It is not the arrangement of the objects but their autonomy that is the paramount feature. The hand that projects into the picture recalls, not least in the way it is designed, the hand of God in so many medieval paintings in the Romanesque style. This points up all the more intensely the profane banality of the objects in Léger's peculiar iconography.

THE TREE

Painted 1925. Oil on canvas, 25 5/8 × 19 5/8''
Sprengel Collection, Hanover

This composition is based on a few representational elements—a house with two black windows, a gray tree that reaches up on both sides of an arcade, an iron railing, three gray hills. There is also, on the left-hand edge of the picture, an unidentifiable checker design deriving from a still extant pencil study. What breathes life into the whole is the contrasts of grisaille and brown planes, of straight lines and curves, of architectural and vegetable elements. Motifs we are familiar with from earlier works are the slippery tree that recalls Henri Rousseau's tropical vegetation, the gray hills, and the railing. A merely secondary motif in the Animated Landscapes, the tree has now become the central theme. There is not a leaf nor a trace of green, but only the greasy-looking trunk and the branches that rear up like snakes or arabesques. Nature is seen as a collection of a few animate and inanimate objects—a sort of "still life."

The picture is pervaded by the soundless poetry of a snowscape and a serene lyricism seldom found in Léger's work. But even here it was not for sentimental reasons that he renounced objectivity and accuracy in the application of the formal mediums.

COMPOSITION WITH LEAF

Painted 1927. Oil on canvas, 51 × 38 1/8"
Musée National Fernand Léger, Biot

The urge to isolate objects led Léger to take another step forward. Every element that gives a picture the quality of a self-contained still life had to be foregone, including the table top on which the objects are posed. Léger himself spoke of a new period of "objects in space": "I made the objects in space in order to be sure of my objects. I felt that I could not put my object on a table without lessening its value as an object. . . . I took the object, got rid of the table, placed the object in the air without perspective or support."

True, at the start he did not quite "place it in the air." One might say he involved it in the taut articulation of the picture. In *Composition with Leaf* the articulation is very like the geometrical arrangement of his abstract murals. It includes a large leaf, a twig with leaves, the back of a playing card, and two crossed objects that look like dumbbells —all things that have no logical association. One can apply to the plant forms what Léger wrote about the flowers

in his pictures: "With the flowers it was quite another matter. They interested me only by way of contrast. Never a flower as a flower, but only when its presence alongside another object creates an unexpected contrast." That— and not from a sentimental angle—is how we must view the flower in the girl's hand in *The Readers* (colorplate 22) and also the plantlike objects in *Composition with Leaf*. The objects are juxtaposed by virtue of their pictorial character, in a purely pictorial relationship, and so perform a decorative function. In Léger's eyes the function of a picture is to bring a dead wall to life; he had nothing against decorative art as such. If in his oeuvre the decorative element became increasingly important, it was because of his conviction that the artist's natural task is to adorn walls. Indeed, it was a growing interest in the architectural function of art that led him to intensify the decorative element in his pictorial language, particularly in the large compositions, where it was linked with a far more general message.

MONA LISA WITH KEYS

Painted 1930. Oil on canvas, 35 7/8 × 28 3/8"
Musée National Fernand Léger, Biot

Léger truly placed his objects "in the air" in 1930 in *Mona Lisa with Keys*. There for the first time the notion of "objects in space" was actually realized. They have been deprived not only of the support of the tabletop but also of the firm articulation of the picture. Before a cloudlike background the objects—the image of Mona Lisa, a bunch of keys, a tin of sardines, a circular form, and a black ribbon that winds round the picture in a heraldic, ornamental fashion—float freely in space.

Léger tells the story of how he got the idea for this picture. "One day, after drawing a bunch of keys, I asked myself what element was furthest removed from the bunch of keys, and I said to myself: 'It's the human face.' I went out into the street and saw in a shop window the portrait of Mona Lisa. That is how I did the picture *Mona Lisa with Keys*, which won a certain celebrity. No contrast has ever been sharper than between this bunch of keys and Mona Lisa." He told the same story on another occasion, adding: "Afterward I also added a tin of sardines. That made an extraordinarily sharp contrast! I am keeping the picture for myself, it's not for sale. . . . I have done the most 'risky' picture as far as contrasting objects are concerned—since for me Mona Lisa is an object like any other. For me this picture, despite the enormous difficulty, is an artistic success."

As if to prove that in his eyes Mona Lisa was "an object like any other," he painted a second picture in which a bunch of keys is associated with a girl who dances floating in space.

Léger's *Mona Lisa with Keys* calls to mind Lautréamont's famous dictum about the beauty of "the chance encounter of an umbrella and a sewing machine on an operating table," which was often quoted by the Surrealists at that time. But what they took as a symbol of the irrationality of dreams and hallucinations was for Léger merely the evidence of a pictorial fact. What attracted him was not the irrational combination of things that have no rational relationship, but the most extreme contrast of pictorial values possible. Nonetheless, we may assume that when he painted the picture Léger was not quite unmindful of Lautréamont's words. In fact, there is a later work along the same lines which shows an umbrella next to the keys.

There is no question of Léger's having the slightest intention of profaning the very essence of museum art, infringing a cultural taboo, or committing a sacrilege, as did Marcel Duchamp with his bearded Mona Lisa of 1919. But all the same one cannot exclude the possibility that the lure of desecration was also involved. Mona Lisa is utilized as a meaningless cliché, and her confrontation with such unhallowed objects as a bunch of keys and a tin of sardines is rather *infra dig*. If this sort of demonstration against "good taste" is a side effect, Mona Lisa plays a positive part—as a sensational formal contrast and even as a dream element one cannot overlook—in the impression made by the picture.

WOMAN BATHING

Painted 1931. Oil on canvas, 38 1/8 × 51''
Private collection, Paris

This picture is one of the landscapes with figures Léger painted in 1931. They have very little in common with the Animated Landscapes of a decade earlier: gone are the mechanical structure and motion of the robot-like figures. The large female figures Léger painted then have lost their hieratic austerity: this *Woman Bathing* resembles the *Three Women* (colorplate 19) only in that she looks straight at the spectator. Also, a comparison with the seated central figure in *The Readers* of 1924 (colorplate 22) shows the difference very clearly. In the later work the ceremonial fixity has disappeared and the whole figure is dynamic; the arms and legs are arched, the anatomical forms—though their volumes are still exaggerated—are less schematic and more organic; the hair is no longer represented by a stereotype form but flows freely over the shoulders, ending in loose strands.

The landscape, too, is very different from the Animated Landscapes of 1920 and thereabouts. It has cast off its geometric shackles to become more harmonious and organic; it now spreads without a break to the horizon and can dispense with such civilizing contrasts as factory buildings and posters. Like the organic forms, it is no longer schematic; in place of the monotonous hillocks there is an undulating plane in the foreground and a varied chain of mountains in the distance; and over all, instead of the pall of factory smoke, a cloudless blue sky. One is put in mind of the Italian Quattrocento; Léger's trip to Italy in 1924 may have had some connection with the change.

Thus, in this picture we find two elements Léger had previously avoided at all costs—the continuum of the human anatomy and the continuum of space. Till now he had done all he could to disrupt the organic context of the human body and build it up of separate, independent, motionless pieces. In the same way he had destroyed the continuum of space by various formal interventions. This *Woman Bathing*, in which he first renounced these principles, marks the beginning of a new period in his art.

Therefore it is not insignificant that at about this same time Léger felt the urge to draw trees, roots, and stones with the greatest possible precision. He confessed that flowers did not interest him as such but were employed merely to provide contrasts in the picture. Trees, rather, fascinated him by their vitality, their strength, and the variety of their forms. This new interest in vegetable growth is reflected in the tree that rises like a green rock beside the naked girl, with only two leafy branches springing from its almost withered trunk. "I remember," Léger wrote, "the play of the moonlight on the felled plane trees, a frightful sight. It was horrible, hellish! They looked like slaughtered beasts. There were branches that screamed. Sometimes, instead, they are so calm! But they only serve without their leaves. No two are alike. I am crazy about trees! I cannot keep still when there are trees around me, such is the temptation to paint them. But I know that I shall never be able to paint them as I see them. How can one give them more expression than they have already?" And, in another context: "I stand before a landscape composed of trees, sky, clouds. I shall concentrate on the tree alone, study it and extract from it all its plastic potentialities: its bark, which often has an expressive pattern; its branches, whose rhythm is dynamic; its leaves, which can have a decorative value. In the picture this tree, so rich in plastic values, is sacrificed to the subject. Isolated and studied on its own, it will provide material for renovating the pictorial expression of our time."

Yet one cannot overlook the fact that in this picture Léger is not interested in the objects alone. They are not treated in such isolation nor in so completely "personalized" a fashion as before; they have come to be components of a general nature poem. The subject Léger so long reviled begins to achieve an important place in his work. The transformation process can be traced back to the pictures with large figures he painted after 1920, and even to *Nudes in the Forest* of 1909–10 (colorplate 1)—in other words, to the very start. Léger himself spoke of *l'inquiétude du sujet*—his concern with the subject—and from here on he became increasingly reconciled with the idea of its having a place in his art.

(BOTTOM)

COLORPLATE 29

TWO SISTERS

Painted 1935. Oil on canvas, 63 3/4 × 44 7/8"
Louis Carré et Cie., Paris

Was it two ugly women that Léger wanted to paint in this picture? What led him to forgo the grace of slender bodies and give his girls such ponderous forms? An important reason was, no doubt, that he was anxious to eliminate competition with the beauty that already existed in nature. The expressive force of the picture had to be independent of the beauty of the female form. Léger was convinced that an artist should avoid flawless beauty. "If an object or a subject is beautiful, it is no longer a raw material but an artistic value in its own right, and therefore useless. One can only observe and admire." Besides, he preferred anti-harmony to harmony, and he despised "good taste."

That Léger made his two girls "ugly" on purpose is made clear by the fact that their bodies are rendered in a more natural fashion than in his earlier pictures. One is tempted to see them as naturalistic in contrast to the more plastic forms of *The Readers* (colorplate 22) or the *Three Figures* (colorplate 23) of 1924. The girls' postures are more relaxed, their forms more organic and tumid. Their limbs are no longer built up of separate pieces, and their movements are regulated not by a mechanism but by the entire organism. Nonetheless, this organic quality is limited by the lack of anatomical definition and the hypertrophic forms, particularly the hands, whose four fingers are quite incapable of holding a flower. The flower in question is inserted in the claw or, rather, added as a contrast to the figures and is only seemingly grasped; in any case, it is less ceremonial than the flowers held by the girl in *The Readers*. The arms seem heavier and more awkward than those in *Three Figures* because they give the im-

pression of being arms, not forms. Lastly, the faces, though still sketchy and masklike, are more modeled and not so spherical as in the pictures of 1924. The frontal posture is also less rigid. This greater naturalness makes us see in the two girls not abstract "figures" but—as the title says—two sisters or, better still, twins.

Having rendered the bodies more naturally, Léger seems to have felt the need to add to their strangeness by painting them a leaden hue and setting them against an abstract yellow background. The *Woman Bathing* of 1931 (colorplate 28) sits in a landscape that, despite her monumental proportions, relates her to the environment; here, the neutral background of *Two Sisters* gives the figures an absolute, monumental quality.

The motif of the flower in the hand of one of the girls forms a striking contrast with the ponderousness of the two figures. This lyrical accent is all the more effective in a milieu pervaded by force. Despite Léger's deep concern for pure pictorial language and his care not to weaken the purity and force of that language for the sake of poetic effect, this picture breathes a poetic spirit that the more severe, inaccessible figure pieces of an earlier period lack entirely—a spirit that stems from the union of violence and tenderness, of reality and unreality.

Fifteen years later, in 1950, Léger employed the same motif of the two girls almost unchanged in the picture entitled *Three Sisters*, in which he added a reclining figure with a boy on her lap playing the accordion, and set the whole group against a blue backdrop.

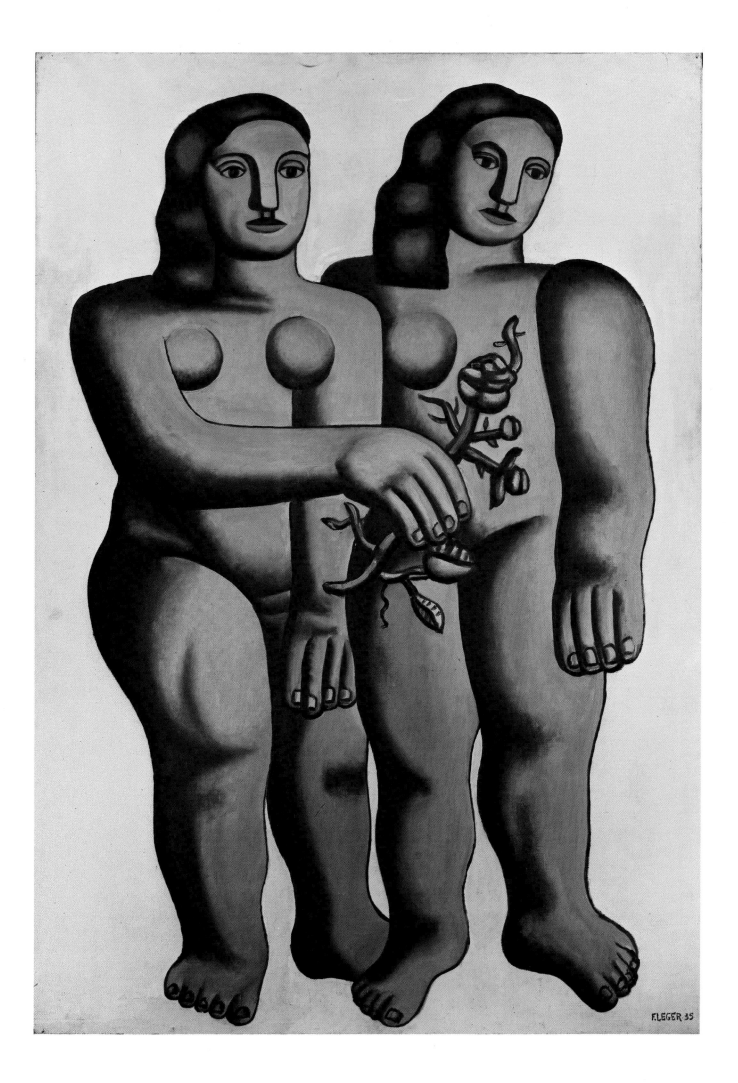

ADAM AND EVE

Painted 1935–39. Oil on canvas, 89 3/4 × 127 3/4''
Kunstsammlung Nordrhein-Westfalen, Düsseldorf

"I am taking up a grand subject," Léger said, "but, I repeat, my painting is still object-painting. It starts about 1936 with *Adam and Eve*. My figures continue to grow more human but I keep to the plastic fact, no eloquence, no romanticism." In spite of his allegiance to the "object" there is no doubt that Léger was increasingly attracted by the "grand subject." Evidence of this is provided by the two monumental works he was busy on simultaneously between 1935 and 1939—*Adam and Eve* and *Composition with Two Parrots* (fig. 34). During the same period he also designed large murals: in 1935 for the Brussels World's Fair, in 1937 for the Palais de la Découverte at the Paris World's Fair. The idea of monumental painting was naturally associated with the idea of architecture and therefore of "the people," for whom this collective art, already socially integrated or aimed to be socially integrated, was intended. Léger was well aware of the problem of collective art and was far from forswearing the easel picture to achieve that objective. "The easel picture still exists—and will always exist—but it can be expanded by the renaissance of the mural."

The big picture *Adam and Eve* was preceded by a smaller version painted in 1934. And a year earlier still, *Marie the Acrobat* already shows the figure of a young woman, though only half-length, with her arm arched above her head; there are also clouds and a stand with clothes. Obviously *Adam and Eve* represents a couple of acrobats; this is confirmed by the reappearance of the rod we know from *Three Figures* of 1924 (colorplate 23), the man's vest, and the design tattooed on his arm. What induced the artist to give the picture the title we know it by may have been the unaffected naiveté of the two figures; the serpent writhing around the rod is a palpable allusion to the theme. Otherwise, it is clear that Léger had no intention of illustrating a story from the Bible.

The two human beings are of the same stock as the *Two Sisters* of 1935 (colorplate 29); though stereotypes frontally arranged, they are more natural, organic, pliant, and lifelike than the *Three Figures* of eleven years before. The odd, "affected" posture of the arms, ponderous yet graceful, derives from *Woman Bathing* of 1931 (colorplate 28) and, more directly, from the dancing girl in *Composition with Three Figures* of 1932. This latter was the point of departure for *Composition with Two Parrots*, in which the idea of dancers is associated with the idea of acrobats.

The picture is divided into two parts after the manner of *Woman Bathing*: on the right, the two figures; on the left, the deliberately badly—but plastically—drawn stand with the blue clothes. In *Woman Bathing* the two halves of the picture are at once separated and linked by the pyramid of blue clothes; here the same function is performed by the rich, colored plant in the woman's hand, which prefigures the flower in *Two Sisters*. This is another instance of Léger's custom, once he had invented a motif, of utilizing it again and again in different contexts.

Slowly and laboriously, in drawings and paintings, he worked up to his big compositions.

Let's take our time. In this rapid, multiform life that hustles us and cuts us in pieces, we must have the strength to stay slow and calm, to work outside the dissolving elements that surround us. To conceive life in its slow, tranquil sense. A work of art needs a temperate climate if it is to be realized to the full. In the increased speed that is the law of the modern world, we must establish fixed points, hang on to them, and labor slowly at the work of the future.

In his early days Léger had glorified the tempo of modern life and taken it as the theme of his art. Now he dissociated himself from it, and this newly found relaxed attitude gave the compositions of the thirties—the thundery period just before the outbreak of World War II—their ample rhythm. With increasing lucidity and resolution Léger took his place in the classical tradition of large-scale figure painting before and after the Italian Renaissance. "The artists of the Italian Renaissance," he said, "copied the human body. For modern painters the problem is entirely different. I, personally, 'invent' the human form more freely than the artists of the Renaissance did. My tradition would be the Romanesque art of the cathedrals and the early art that preceded the Italian Renaissance." And in another context: "People will realize later that this new art is not very revolutionary, that it is linked with the ancient tradition against which it had to fight and from which it had to break free and stand on its own feet."

TWO WOMEN WITH A BIRD

Painted 1942. Oil on canvas, 45 5/8 × 35 1/2''
Collection Jan Österlöf, Stockholm

World War II broke out in 1939. In October of the following year Léger emigrated to the United States, which he had visited for the first time in 1931. There he stayed, teaching at Yale University and elsewhere, until his return to France in December, 1945.

Fascinated as he was by the forms and tempo of modern life, Léger could not help being greatly impressed by New York, which he called "the most colossal spectacle on earth." He was overwhelmed by the "apotheosis of vertical architecture" and by the bridges and lights of the metropolis. "The rigor of the architecture shattered by the limitless fantasy of the colored lights. . . . Mechanical life has its apogee there. . . . Architecture and light are the two poles of their plastic expression. . . . I love this spectacular excess, this unbridled force."

In spite of Léger's enthusiasm for the American scene, there is, properly speaking, no "American Period" in his oeuvre. He himself insisted on the unbroken continuity of his art: "My work continues and develops independently of my geographical position. . . . My environment does not affect me in the least. A work of art is the result of an inner condition and owes nothing to picturesque appearances. Perhaps the rhythm or the climate of New York enables me to work faster. That's all."

Léger did, however, have a visual experience to which he attributed a strong impact on his art. *Two Women with a Bird* of 1942 may be mentioned as an example. This is how he described it: "In 1942, in the streets of New York—on Broadway, to be exact—I was struck by the colored lights that the advertisements flash on the streets. I was talking with someone. His face was blue; twenty seconds later it turned yellow. That color went, another came, and it turned red, then green. I raised my eyes and looked at the buildings. They were sawed in colored strips. I was greatly impressed. That color, the color of the flashing lights, was free—free in space. I tried to do the same thing in my pictures."

One can readily understand that Léger's imagination was fired by this experience and that, of all those that assaulted his consciousness in New York, it is the one he seized upon. The spectacle was more than a great surprise; it accorded with his own deep-seated urge to free color. There, outside his art, in the real world, was color loosed from all representational ties. The immediate outcome was that he decided to divorce design and color in his pictures. This he carried out in *Two Women with a Bird*, in which he drew the outlines of faces, hands, and a parrot over a few broad bands of color that give the picture plane a stable, though no longer geometric, support. "I separated the color completely from the design; that gives a quite different movement, an intense dynamism." Color became entirely autonomous, and objects and figures, colorless and deprived of volume, were thrust back into their linear contours. This produced an extremely strong contrast in his work, a new feature that Léger employed in several pictures, including *The Great Parade* of 1954 (colorplate 40), in which figural scenes are drawn in black lines over broad patches of independent color.

THE DIVERS II

Painted 1941–42. Oil on canvas, 90 × 68"
The Museum of Modern Art, New York City
Mrs. Simon Guggenheim Fund

The theme of *The Divers* was developed in a great many studies and paintings between 1940 and 1945. Léger himself tells us how that came about:

> In 1940 I was working on my *Divers* in Marseilles. Five or six men diving. I left for the United States and one day went to a swimming pool there. The divers were no longer five or six but two hundred at once. Just try and find yourself! Whose is that head? Whose that leg? Whose those arms? I hadn't a clue. So I scattered the limbs in my picture. I think I was far closer to the truth in that than Michelangelo was when he studied the detail of the muscles of each limb. I have seen the figures he painted in the Sistine Chapel: they don't fall, they stay put in all the corners of the buildings. One can distinguish their toenails. I assure you that when those fellows in Marseilles jumped into the water I had no time to observe the details, and my divers really fall.

Léger's interest in falling bodies is surprising in view of his propensity for classical balance and calm, particularly in figure pieces. Perhaps the reason is that, after treating "objects in space," he was now attracted by "figures in space." About his Divers he said: "This is a dynamic cycle that obliges me to project groups of human figures into space." They float freely without any ground-level support and almost without any difference between up and down. In this version the bodies form an inextricable tangle of limbs with a scattering of heads, in which Léger "found time" to record fingernails and toenails. For, of course, what he had said about there being no time to observe details of that sort was merely a pretext to criticize Michelangelo's naturalism. It was not because he lacked time but, on the contrary, because he took time that he painted certain details while neglecting others for artistic reasons.

That Léger's figures, unlike Michelangelo's, really fall is only a part truth and is contradicted by the fact that his pictures may be virtually turned upside down. Léger's static sensibility enabled him to combine the cascading bodies in a stable composition where gravitation acts toward the center rather than the bottom of the picture. The limbs wave in all directions—only the heads point downward—and the general impression is of more a circular than a vertical motion. Lastly, the colored ground also acts as a brake on the motion and not as a wall before which the bodies fall. The entire cycle of Divers—in which different pictures employ very different procedures—has a static quality that recalls fresco painting; what dynamism the pictures display is due more to the agitated forms than to the falling bodies.

The figures are painted in grisaille, calling to mind the gray humanity in the pictures of about 1920. The lively interchange of light and dark has the dual task of rendering volume and movement. Strongly contrasted with this is the polychrome ground, composed of abstract forms painted red, yellow, blue, green, and black, without a trace of painterly shading. The contour is to these forms what the modeling is to the bodies. The drawing of the figures is dissociated from the autonomous colors as in *Two Women with a Bird* of the same year (colorplate 31), but in a different manner. In other paintings of this cycle Léger adopted the same procedure as in this latter work: the bands of color applied freely on the canvas serve as a foil to the figures of the divers, which are merely outlined (see also fig. 39).

THREE MUSICIANS

Painted 1944. Oil on canvas, 68 1/2 × 57 1/4"
The Museum of Modern Art, New York City
Mrs. Simon Guggenheim Fund

In 1921 Picasso painted his two big pictures of *Three Musicians* in a flat Cubist style resembling collage that persisted alongside contemporary works in a more classical manner. In 1930 Léger took up the theme in the first version of his *Three Musicians*, which was followed by a second fourteen years later. In addition, there are many studies and paintings in which the trio forms part of a more ample composition. This is in keeping with Léger's custom of utilizing his pictorial inventions in various combinations.

Léger turned Picasso's musicians into rustic players—three men with accordion, trombone, and double bass, dressed in their Sunday best complete with hat, red waistcoat, collar, and necktie; the trombone player also wears a badge on his lapel. Though the three men are stereotypes, they are rendered more freely than in the first version, which was painted in the pedantic manner of the late twenties. Their naive appearance and attitudes recall Henri Rousseau, but of course Léger's naiveté was the result not of a natural bent but of his sympathy with the common man.

Léger had loved the common people ever since he "discovered" them in the trenches in 1914. Though he took an artistic interest in the ballet and the drama, he preferred popular shows to those of the "great world." He repeatedly voiced his admiration for "the wonderful masses of the people, whose instinct is right. . . . One must," he said, "at all costs avoid debilitated societies (the middle class, the effete aristocracy). There is nothing to gain and everything to lose. . . . The common people, with their coarse, tough manner, tragic and comic, always exaggerated, are the proper class for us. I personally live among them as much as I can and feel happy there."

Léger saw a surprising connection between the language of the people and the language of modern art: "It is those people who every day invent a verbal poetry that is constantly renovated, namely, slang. Their creative imagination is always awake. They transpose reality. What else do modern artists, poets, and painters do? They do exactly the same thing. Our pictures are our slang. We transpose objects, forms, colors. So why shouldn't we get together?"

But he was well aware—and it was one of his preoccupations—that getting together was a one-sided affair. He could not count on simple people to appreciate a picture like *Three Musicians*, in which he depicted their simplicity. In the large figure pieces painted during the last years of his life he endeavored to bridge the tragic gulf with the utopian ideal of an "earthly paradise."

BIG JULIE

Painted 1945. Oil on canvas, 44 × 50 1/8"
The Museum of Modern Art, New York City
Acquired through the Lillie P. Bliss Bequest

An essay Léger wrote in 1952 entitled "How I Conceive the Figure" begins with these words: "One might just as well change the title and replace it with 'The Bunch of Keys in Léger's Oeuvre' or 'The Bicycle in Léger's Oeuvre.' This means that for me the human figure and the human body are no more important than keys or bikes."

This statement is both confirmed and contradicted by *Big Julie*. Confirmed, because the bicycle and the human figure are depicted on the same scale and given the same importance, just as the bunch of keys and the Mona Lisa were in the picture of 1930 (colorplate 27). Contradicted, because the figure of Julie seems less like an object than Mona Lisa in the earlier painting, whose figure was taken, typically, from a picture postcard. Léger's conversion from the object to the subject is reflected in the more "human" and at the same time more monumental vision of the human figure; the latter is still an object only insofar as it continues to be ruled by the picture law.

Léger celebrated the bicycle not only in its banality as a commonplace object but also as the favorite vehicle for people's trips in the country; it is more than a neutral object, interesting only for its pictorial value. This is true not only in *Big Julie* but also in such later works as *Les Belles Cyclistes*, *A Fine Team*, and *Homage to Louis David* (colorplate 36). As for the girl, she is not simply an element of the composition as was Mona Lisa—and treated ironically in the bargain—but the symbol of the strong, healthy, forward-looking young members of the working class.

The picture was painted in America in 1945, shortly before Léger returned to France. He admitted that without the experience of America he would not have painted his girl cyclists. "Bad taste is one of this country's basic qualities. Bad taste, glaring colors: here the painter must reorganize everything and can make full use of his skill. Girls in sweaters, with vivid makeup; girls in shorts, turned out like circus acrobats. If I had seen only girls dressed in good taste, I would never have painted my cyclists and, in particular, my *Big Julie*." How fond he was of his girl cyclists is proved by what he said one day in a restaurant, looking out on the street: "There they are, my *Belles Cyclistes*, with Big Julie in the middle. Health, life, forms, colors. They spew out the dust of office or factory and drink in the air of the open country. One can build something with forces like those." What he wanted to see built was not pictures but the human society.

Big Julie is divided vertically into two halves. The girl stands before a black ground, the heraldically deformed cycle before a brown cross painted on a yellow ground. This cross recalls Malevich's late pictures. Needless to say, the yellow flower in the girl's hand and the two blue butterflies serve chiefly as contrast, but they also symbolize the "country air" that the girls breathed on their weekend excursions.

THE ACROBAT AND HIS PARTNER

Painted 1948. Oil on canvas, 51 × 63 3/4''
Galerie Maeght, Paris

Léger had a lifelong love for the circus. During the years that preceded World War I, he used to go to the Cirque Médrano in Paris with his poet friends Guillaume Apollinaire, Max Jacob, and Blaise Cendrars. In New York he was a fan of Barnum's three-ring circus in Madison Square Garden. *Le Cirque*, which he wrote and illustrated in 1949, is a paean in praise of the ring and therefore a rejection of the geometricality of the right angle:

Since the earth is round, how can you play square? . . . Life is a circuit. You start out on a journey, but you come back to your starting point. . . . I have often dreamed of a round architecture and of living in spheres. . . . Nothing is so round as the circus. It is a huge basin where circular forms develop. . . . A circus is a rotation of volumes, people, animals, and objects. The awkward, dry angle is not at home there. . . . Go to the circus! You leave behind your rectangles, your geometrical windows, and enter the land of circles in action. It is so human to break through limits, to grow bigger, to push out toward freedom. . . . The ring is free; it has neither beginning nor end. High up, two trapeze artistes in yellow and pink tights catch the light. The human body, moving in all directions, viewed foreshortened from below, rolls pleasantly in its skin-tight costume.

The background to the acrobatic turn, a vast, target-like circle striped red, yellow, blue, white, and green, is a distant echo of *The Disks* of 1918 (colorplate 13) and of Delaunay's *formes circulaires*. But what we have here is not a geometrical disk but the round circus ring. In the foreground is the boldly foreshortened figure of the artiste with a flower in his hand, revolving yet stationary. His partner stands motionless by his side, holding a ladder. There is also a chair with a gray cat, the whole framed by an ornamental arrangement of structural and floral forms.

This is what Léger himself wrote about the picture: "In *The Acrobat and His Partner* the acrobat and the disk that surrounds him represent movement. The flower in his hand, composed entirely of curves, heightens the impression of movement; so does the shape of the cat on the chair. The straight lines of the chair, those at the edge of the canvas on the same side, the ladder, and the acrobat's partner form the static part of the picture, which contrasts violently with the dynamic part. The more contrasts there are in a picture, the stronger is the painting. Less contrasts there are, and the more melodious it is: I am antimelodious.

The picture lacks any trace of the big-top atmosphere. Even in such a setting Léger's art has neither atmosphere nor mood nor nervous vibration: he never saw any reason to modify his pictorial language and adapt it to a motif. Even the lure of the circus could not alter its matter-of-fact lucidity.

The figure of the twisting acrobat recurs in a picture of 1953 together with a juggler and an equestrienne; another, painted in 1955, shows the girl vaulting over the horse's back. Léger, like so many of his fellow artists, busied himself with the circus motif for years. The *Woman Bathing* of 1931 (colorplate 28), with her twisted arms and legs, might be a precursor of his circus cycle; its culmination was *The Great Parade* of 1954 (colorplate 40).

(BOTTOM)

HOMAGE TO LOUIS DAVID (LES LOISIRS)

Painted 1948–49. Oil on canvas, 60 5/8 × 73"
Musée National d'Art Moderne, Paris

The scene is a conventional composition arranged after the manner of a family photograph: wearing a fixed smile on their lips, the people face the spectator in a carefully posed group. The men are of the same stock as the *Three Musicians* (colorplate 33); the girls are like *Big Julie* (colorplate 34).

Léger had finally evolved his working-class type, and he used it for acrobats in the circus or picnickers in the country, as his need dictated. It is the ideal plain man, lighthearted and self-satisfied—a type that expressed the artist's idealistic hope in the future brotherhood of mankind and his faith in a free, classless, nonviolent society, as reflected in so many of his lectures and essays. "We are advancing, I trust, toward a novel, slightly dangerous form of humane, luminous, transparent society." Léger insisted again and again, especially after World War II, on the notion of that kind of earthly paradise. His native positivism was linked with a social utopianism, and he was convinced that art had a mission to perform: "Look! How beautiful our world is! The new art brings peace and happiness."

The artist gave this picture of urban vacationers taking their ease in the country the surprising title of *Homage to Louis David*. Though there is no apparent relationship, by dedicating it to the great classical painter of the French Revolution and the Napoleonic era he thus celebrated David's sober, Republican austerity; the unromantic, unsentimental quality of his art; the clear, architectonic composition of his pictures. Léger always claimed descent from the tradition of antiquity and the early Middle Ages. Here, for once, he stretched out his hand to a representative of the despised historical painting of the early nineteenth century.

> I wanted to mark my return to simplicity by a direct, unsubtle art that everyone can understand. . . . I loved David because he is anti-impressionistic. He achieved the utmost that can be obtained from imitation and that is why his pictures are completely lacking in the atmosphere of the Renaissance. I feel David, particularly in his portraits, far closer to me than Michelangelo. I love the dryness in David's work and in Ingres's too. That was my way and it touched me at once.

And in another context: "There is a terrain that we have avoided. David. I am returning to him."

In his younger days Léger celebrated the modern world of work. Now that he was more interested in people, he celebrated rest and recreation as the expression of freedom and happiness. This is mirrored not only in the scene as a whole but also in the motley clothes and smiling faces of the people he has portrayed, in the bicycles, the gay colors, the flowers, the blue sky, and the doves in the clouds. At that time the dove was taken as the symbol of peace by the Communist party, of which Léger was a member; and in 1949, the year when this picture was finished, Picasso produced for the party the lithograph of his dove, which is actually too personal to be a valid symbol. In Léger's picture the doves seem to be a symbolic confirmation of the earthly happiness he so greatly prized.

COLORPLATE 37

THE CONSTRUCTORS

Painted 1950. Oil on canvas, 118 × 78 3/4"
Musée National Fernand Léger, Biot

When Léger took up the theme of construction workers in 1940, it looked as if he was reverting to the technical, mechanical world of his youth. But his attitude to that world was very different from what it had been thirty years before. Then he celebrated the glory of modern technology, which he placed above humanity; now, in the Constructors series, man asserts his freedom even in the face of technological constraint. The technoid, robot-like puppets of 1920 have become natural human beings, and the artist has gone so far as to bestow on them some individual features. Man no longer obeys the laws of technology but only the less strict, more relaxed law of the picture. Nonetheless, the artist still maintained his position that man is the "object" of the picture and not its paramount "subject." If Léger felt the need to give him greater individuality, it was to strengthen the contrast with the rigid metal structures. What interested him first was pictorial contrast, and only secondarily the more natural representation of the human being.

In 1950 and 1951 Léger devoted many oils, drawings, and gouaches to the theme of construction workers in action surrounded by steel girders (see figs. 42, 43). The most important was executed in 1950, but it was followed the next year by others, which included drawings of heads, hands, legs, and details of figures. This means that the drawings were done after the painting, and one cannot help being surprised by the deep interest Léger took in details that disappear in the painting's schematic handling.

The artist has given us a detailed account of how he came to paint the picture. "When I built *The Constructors*, I did not make a single plastic concession. I got the idea traveling to Chevreuse by road every evening. A factory was under construction in the fields there. I saw the men swaying high up on the steel girders! I saw man like a flea; he seemed still lost in his inventions with the sky above him. I wanted to render that; the contrast between man and his inventions, between the worker and all

that metal architecture, that hardness, that ironwork, those bolts and rivets. The clouds, too, I arranged technically, but they form a contrast with the girders. No concession to sentimentality, even if my figures are more varied and individual. I try to do something new without leaving aside the problem. In my work humanity has evolved like the sky. I set more store on the existence of the people but at the same time I control their actions and their passions. I think that in this way truth is expressed better, more directly, more durably. The anecdote ages quickly."

It would have been Léger's dream to paint his pictures of workers for the workers themselves. He was constantly preoccupied with the problem of how the modern artist could get in touch with the people. He spoke of the "profound drama that separates the modern artist from the people, who yet are so instinctive and creative." By raising that question he thought he had "touched the dramatic, central point which interests us all and which we must all try to solve." With a view to tackling the problem at first hand, he exhibited his *Constructors* in the canteen of the Renault automobile factory. This is how he describes the result: "The men arrived at noon. They looked at the pictures while they ate. Some of them laughed. 'Look at those guys, they'll never be able to work with hands like that!' In a word, they judged by comparison. They found my pictures funny. They didn't understand them. I listened to them and gulped down my soup sadly. A week later I went back to the canteen for a meal. The atmosphere had changed. The men didn't laugh any more, they no longer bothered about the pictures. But quite a few of them, as they ate, looked up at my pictures for a moment and then lowered their eyes again to their plate. Maybe the pictures puzzled them? As I was leaving, one of the men said to me: 'You're the painter, aren't you? You'll see, when your pictures are taken away and they are faced with a blank wall, my buddies will realize what's in your colors.' That sort of thing is gratifying."

120

TWO GIRLS ON BICYCLES

Painted 1951. Oil on canvas, 63 3/4 × 45"
Galerie Maeght, Paris

In 1942, under the impact of the flashing colored lights of Broadway, Léger began to free color from all representational fetters, spread it on the canvas in broad bands and patches, and do the drawing freely over it. He employed this separation of line and color in a number of works, though by no means systematically, right up to the end of his life. In *Two Girls on Bicycles* of 1951 the ground consists of large patches of color; but those colors do not keep in the background: they irradiate the whole scene, which only holds its own thanks to the strong contour lines. The group formed by the mother and child is the same as the one in the large *Homage to Louis David* of 1948–49 (colorplate 36). Now, however, the open country and blue sky have been replaced by a flat, brightly colored plane. It is typical of Léger that he did not abandon a theme after using it to perfection in a large composition; he could not help taking it up again and again in a different shape or, as here, with a different technique. In the case in point, if we compare the earlier picture with this one, we may find the group slightly more anecdotic and hemmed in by the genre-like narrative, whereas here it is treated with a grandeur that recalls fresco painting.

THE COUNTRY OUTING

Painted 1954. Oil on canvas, 94 1/2 × 118''
Fondation Maeght, Saint-Paul-de-Vence

Édouard Manet created a sensation in 1863 with *Le Dé-jeuner sur l'herbe*, a picture of two men and a naked woman sitting on the grass, with another woman bathing in the background. Léger must have had that famous work in mind when he painted his *Country Outing* ninety years later, for he revered Manet as one of the greatest innovators in the history of art. But if we except the group of three figures and the idyllic rural setting, the two paint-ers have nothing at all in common. Léger's men do not be-long to the artistic milieu; they are more like members of the provincial working class. In his landscape there is no trace of romantic charm; Manet's huge trees have been replaced by one bare tree whose few branches bear a few skinny leaves. In every other respect, the means of artistic expression employed by the two artists is so different that no comparison is possible.

Léger had been preoccupied by the theme of the coun-try outing since 1943, when he did a pen drawing in which, as in Manet's picture, trees still occupied an important place. That study was followed by many others, but the tree was thrust more and more into the background. After executing the first version of his *Country Outing* (1953), Léger continued to work on the motif, as was his wont, keeping the patches of color separate from the drawing. This practice was employed in the second major version of 1953, whose scene is enriched by the addition of a man working under the open bonnet of a car.

Compared with *Homage to Louis David* of five years before (colorplate 36), the postures of the figures have lost much of their ceremonial character, while more stress is laid on their casual, momentary aspect. In *The Con-structors* (colorplate 37) figures were already depicted in profile—a pose that virtually never occurred in Léger's earlier works, with the exception of *The Mechanic* of 1920 (colorplate 16), who is shown in stiff profile after what might be termed the Egyptian fashion. Now there is even a figure—the man working on his car—viewed from behind. This readiness to comply with natural reality is not a sign of weakness but, on the contrary, of increasing strength and assurance; the artist is sure enough of his creative powers to risk a concession to a reality outside the picture. Not for a moment does he run the risk of pan-dering to socialist realism, which is merely naturalism with a socialist theme.

What Léger said about *The Constructors* is also true of this picture: "If I was able to approach very close to a realistic figuration, it was because the violent contrast between my workmen and the metal geometry in which they are set is at its maximum. Modern subjects, whether social or other, are valid insofar as this law of contrasts is respected; otherwise one falls back on the classical picture of the Italian Renaissance." It is true that in *The Country Outing* the contrast motif of the geometrical steel construction work is absent, but there is no lack of other strong contrasts—between the rigid structure of the fence, the petrified form of the tree, and the rounded forms of figures and landscape—and, more particularly, between the patches of violent colors.

THE GREAT PARADE

Painted 1954. Oil on canvas, 117 3/4 × 157 1/2''
The Solomon R. Guggenheim Museum, New York City

Three large colored forms provide stable support for the many figures of this lively picture—a red circle and two broad bands, one blue and horizontal, the other orange and vertical. Where the horizontal band and the circle intersect, in the middle of the canvas, the artist has introduced a big black capital C, the initial letter of the word *Circus.* The three colored areas that underlie the design are abstract forms, but it is clear that the circle symbolizes the circus ring, as it did in *The Acrobat and His Partner* of 1948 (colorplate 35). The festive effect of this colored ground is enhanced by the addition of two small circles, one green, one yellow, and of a yellow rectangle. The scene enacted before it is a parade of acrobats and riders, trapeze artistes and clowns—the final apotheosis of a circus performance and at the same time of Fernand Léger's art. The origins of this picture, too, date back a great many years. The girl lying in the man's arms appears, together with the three musicians, in a drawing of 1940. The same combination occurs in a painting of 1945 and again in a drawing of 1953, which shows how long it was present in the painter's mind. On the other hand, in *The Great Parade* the trio is replaced by a single musical clown, who crops up for the first time in a picture painted in 1941. As the composition slowly matured, Léger introduced many different figures and groups from his repertoire, either provisionally or definitively. As he tells us, "I worked on *The Great Parade* for two years. I study everything ponderously. I work very slowly indeed. I am unable to improvise. The more I watch myself, the more I see that I am a classic. I do a long preparatory work. First I do a quantity of drawings, then I do gouaches, and lastly I pass on to the canvas; but when I tackle that I have 80 percent assurance. I know where I am going."

In another context he said: "If I have drawn circus people, acrobats, clowns, jugglers, it is because I have taken an interest in their work for thirty years. Ever since I designed cubist costumes for the Fratellini. I did a quantity of drawings and studies for *The Great Parade.* For I am a classic: if my first drawings are always done off the cuff, I am aware of the media that I shall employ. A year elapsed between the first version of *The Great Parade* and its final state. This interval corresponds to a lengthy process of elaboration and synthesis. The slightest transformation was long pondered and worked up with the help of new drawings. A local alteration often involved changing the entire composition because it affected the balance of the whole. In the first version the color exactly fitted the forms. In the definitive version one can see what force, what vitality is achieved by using color on its own."

A painter who worked after this fashion was destined for monumental art. It is not only its large size that makes *The Great Parade* a monumental work. A few colored areas comprise the profusion of figures, bodies, and intertwined parts of bodies: this is the language, the spirit, the ample breadth of mural painting.

Large volumes of colors over a large surface. We advance toward the future, and it is a collective future. Yes, some social and artistic signs indicate that we are on the brink of a renaissance of mural art. Monumental art can and must utilize and amplify this new conception. The young architects who are rebuilding Europe have turned their gaze in this direction, they have understood. This art must find its place in vast architectures. We are coming back to what I have already said: It is static in its expression, it respects the wall side by side with a dynamic conception that destroys the wall. It will be not only measure and balance, but invention and rhythm as well.

PHOTOGRAPHIC CREDITS

The author and publisher wish to thank the museums and private collectors for permitting the reproduction of paintings, photographs, and drawings in their collections. Photographs have been supplied by the owners or custodians of the works of art except for the following, whose courtesy is gratefully acknowledged:

Galerie Beyeler (Basel): figs. 12, 17; J. E. Bulloz (Paris): colorplate 13; Geoffrey Clements (New York): colorplates 18, 32–34; Photo Doisneau-Rapho (Paris): frontispiece; Foto Heri (Solothurn): colorplate 23; Michael Hertz (Bremen): fig. 24; Colorphoto Hinz (Basel): colorplates 4, 12, 14, 20; Photo Hubert Josse (Paris): colorplates 28, 29, 39; Walter Klein (Gerresheim): fig. 25; Bert Koch: colorplates 9, 17; Galerie Louise Leiris (Paris): figs. 1, 5, 7–9, 20–23, 28, 30, 31, 33, 36–38, 40, 42, 44, 46; Michel de Lorenzo (Nice): colorplates 21, 26, 27, 37; Studio Jacques Mer (Antibes): figs. 11, 16, 35, 41, 47, 48; O. E. Nelson (New York): fig. 45; Photostudio Otto (Vienna): colorplate 5; Service Photographique (Paris): colorplates 2, 22, 36, figs. 10, 34; Photo Wellard: colorplate 16; Alfred J. Wyatt: colorplate 15.

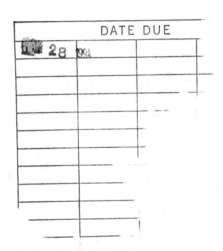